Praise for *The Out-of-Sync Child*
by Carol Kranowitz

This book is great! It is a real contr
many children who are so hard to und
the hook of blaming themselves . . . an
job of addressing the child's underlyin

—T. Berry Brazelton, MD, founder,
Brazelton Touchpoints Center, Boston Children's Hospital

Warm and wise, this book will bring both hope and practical help
to parents who wonder why their kid doesn't "fit in."
—Jane M. Healy, learning specialist and
author of *Your Child's Growing Mind*

The Out-of-Sync Child does a masterful job of describing the different ways children react to sensations and integrate their responses
to their world. The book provides detailed, practical information
that will help parents understand how the nervous system works.
—Stanley I. Greenspan, MD,
child psychiatrist and author (with Serena Wieder)
of *The Child with Special Needs*

Comprehensive yet easy to understand . . . helpful tools for parents
to promote healthy integration.
—*Exceptional Parent*

A "Top Ten Book for Parenting Children with Disabilities."
—*Brain, Child Magazine*

CAROL STOCK KRANOWITZ, MA

The
Out-of-Sync
Child
Grows Up

Coping with Sensory Processing Disorder
in the Adolescent and Young Adult Years

A TarcherPerigee Book

tarcherperigee
An imprint of Penguin Random House LLC
375 Hudson Street
New York, New York 10014

Most TarcherPerigee books are available at special quantity discounts for bulk purchase for sales promotions, premiums, fund-raising, and educational needs. Special books or book excerpts also can be created to fit specific needs. For details, write: SpecialMarkets@penguinrandomhouse.com.

ISBN 9780399176319

Printed in the United States of America
ScoutAutomatedPrintCode

Book design by Spring Hoteling

I Am from SPD

I am from tight hugs and "No touching!"

I am from tastes I love and textures I hate,

I am from no tears over sprained ankles,

I am from nervously pulling out my teeth,

I am from sounds too loud, and lights too bright.

I am from diagnosis and acronyms,

I am from confusion and understanding,

I am from doctors and professionals,

I am from "burrito" swings and speech therapy,

I am from "We don't know what to do,"

I am from "We can do this," and "No, I can't!"

I am from homework too difficult and nights spent crying,

I am from a C feeling like an A,

I am from a C feeling like an F,

I am from love, acceptance, and knowledge,

I am from hating education, to loving knowledge.

I am from self-exploration and creativity,

I am from dandelions in homemade vases and birdhouses painted
   pink and gold.

I am from kicking and screaming,

I am from smiles and laughter.

I am from 19 years of life,

I am from long brown hair, cut, dyed and chopped,

I am from piercing and tattoos,

I am from long nails and brilliant white teeth.

I am from a woman always in flight, a busy working bee,

I am from driving by myself,

I am from holding my first job.

I am from dreaming of normalcy,

I am from anything but normal,

I am from battling the stereotype,

I am from personal victory,

I am from a luck of the draw, a one in a million,

I am from what made the stars.

I am from SPD.

—Hayley Fannin

Hayley is a technical college graduate living in Washington State. She is on the path to find a permanent career, currently working and enjoying life with family and friends by her side.

For the parents who wonder how their children
with SPD will fare in adolescence and young adulthood,

For the preteens and teenagers who wonder
what growing older with SPD will feel like, and

For the brave, honest,
sensational individuals who tell us all about it.

CONTENTS

PART III
COPING WITH RELATIONSHIPS

PART IV
LIVING AN "IN-SYNC" LIFE

FOREWORD

Carol Stock Kranowitz has again hit one out of the stadium with *The Out-of-Sync Child Grows Up*. Since her first book was published in 1998, dozens of occupational therapists and other authors have followed in her footsteps to write books about SPD. Some books are great in different ways—for example, some offer parents more specific strategies, include more research, come with a clinical perspective, discuss IEPs and special education options, or are more relevant for older children and their families. But Carol's book was first, and when parents and teachers get their hands on it and begin to learn about SPD, they are off and running.

Everyone she meets tells her, "You changed my life. I don't know how I would have lived with my SPD kid without your book . . . Thank you so, so much."

Carol is a self-proclaimed occupational therapist "wannabe," which means that she wants to provide OT suggestions to every mom, dad, grandma, grandpa, aunt, and uncle who comes up at one of her presentations and waits thirty minutes to ask her questions about their own child. I have seen her time and time again listen and help the fortunate people who do get to talk to her. She honestly acknowledges the limits of her knowledge as well, never going beyond her scope of practice as a teacher. If she doesn't have an answer or a strategy to suggest, she says, "I don't know, but I'll find out for you," because she knows where to look for it!

The sensory kids who were her preschool students at St. Columba's Nursery School in Washington, DC, are getting older. They are among the approximately 16 percent of the population with SPD (based on a recent epidemiological study funded by the National Institutes of Health). More and more of them have reached adolescence and many are young adults. "Now what?" they and their worried parents are asking. Not only the children she taught, but all children with SPD need guidance and reassurance as they mature.

Because her expertise is with young children, Carol turned to the experts who truly know what it is like to grow up with SPD. She has gathered stories from more than fifty contributors talking about the issues related to having SPD when a "Sensory Kid" becomes a Sensory Adolescent or Adult. The stories touch on life experiences, from getting up in the morning and gearing up for school to going to sleep at night, from putting on clothes to picking out clothes for dating, from being in a family to making your own family, and more.

If you or a loved one has SPD, you cannot miss reading Carol's new book. You'll be glad you made the time for it! You'll be glad to know you are not alone and that people are listening.

As for me, everything that made me who I am, everything that led me into the field of occupational therapy as a researcher and therapist for children and families with SPD, started when I was a teenager. Life threw me a curveball when I began to lose my eyesight at age sixteen. Eventually (at ages twenty and twenty-one), I received some of the first corneal transplants done in this country. Although the disease I had was not SPD, it had some of the same symptoms. Just as it is for adolescents with SPD, functioning in daily life, getting around, studying, participating in social situations—almost everything I needed and wanted to do—became a constant struggle.

Now, slowly losing my sight was bad enough. More defeating was when the ophthalmologist my parents brought me to told them nothing was wrong; it was "all in my head."

Do you know what it feels like being sixteen and having no one believe you? That is enough to make you crazy. Not a little crazy, a lot crazy. You begin to doubt yourself. And once you doubt yourself, you get into a spiral of failure.

For those with SPD, not being believed by doctors, teachers, friends, or parents is a major problem. The lack of understanding by most of society is most hurtful and hard to forgive in a world that gives so little to these youngsters. They crave support, and it is often so very hard to find.

They need to learn resilience, and in Carol's book, most (not all) writers are very resilient. It is hopeful to read so many accounts of teens and adults getting emotional and therapeutic support from some parents, a few teachers and mentors, and some special friends who really listen and really have learned how to help.

Hope and help. What Carol Kranowitz has crafted here offers both. Read it and smile; read it and cry; read it and talk about it.

And you, like me, will thank her once again for another amazing and heartful winner.

—Lucy Jane Miller, PhD, OTR
Founder, STAR Institute for Sensory Processing Disorder

Author of *Sensational Kids: Hope and Help for Children with SPD*
Coauthor of *No Longer A SECRET: Unique Common Sense Strategies for Children with Sensory or Motor Challenges*

April 2016

ABOUT THIS BOOK

This book is about what it feels like to grow up with sensory processing disorder (SPD). It is also about what parents, teenagers, teachers, medical doctors, mental health professionals, occupational therapists, and other interested people can do to make life more enjoyable for preteens, adolescents, and young adults with SPD. The book has five purposes:

Purpose #1: To give adolescents and adults looking back an opportunity to share their stories and voice their feelings about growing up with SPD—perhaps for the first time.

So much courage is required, not only to survive and thrive, but also to talk about SPD!

Purpose #2: To help readers living *with*—or living *as*—an adolescent with SPD to validate their feelings and experiences.

If you are a teenager or a teenager's parent and are feeling overwhelmed by SPD's emotional fallout, getting into the writers' heads may help you make sense of your own emotions, thoughts, and actions. You will see that you are not alone.

TALKING AT LAST ABOUT SPD

Ember Walker

People need to know about SPD. It kind of feels great to get some SPD things that I have dealt with out in the open. Because of how I've been looked at my whole life, I've shared them with nobody other than my family. (I only told them because, well, to live with me, you'd notice some of these things.) For young people growing up, I need to do so now, and I'm glad to share my story and struggle. Apparently, I have a lot to say.

Purpose #3: To give readers a sense of what the future may hold.

You will get a feel for what is possible for an individual with SPD traveling through life. You will learn that you can find outside help and can help yourself—and that the future is full of hope.

Purpose #4: To offer specific coping strategies for SPD.

Parents and adolescents wonder not only what to expect, but also what to do to meet sensory challenges right now. You will hear advice from experts in the business of supporting kids with SPD—mothers and fathers, occupational therapists, and other professionals who treat teenagers and adults with the condition.

Purpose #5: To increase public awareness about SPD.

As SPD and other developmental issues become more prevalent, it becomes increasingly important for everyone, not just people affected directly, to understand and respect individuals with sensory challenges. Those with SPD are all around us. They may be sitting on the couch beside you or working at a desk nearby or living next door.

You needn't live with SPD to notice how the hypersensitive, clumsy, or disorganized behavior of adolescents and young adults with sensory challenges affects you and other people. Would you like to learn how to help them and thus have your classroom, Boy Scout meetings, office, or community at large run more smoothly?

Many of your questions will be answered in this book!

Use this book to learn about the young person that you care for—or perhaps to learn about yourself. Be a detective to find clues and recognize patterns in out-of-sync behavior. For example, a teen's refusal to go to events with friends (because of loud crowds), sudden sleepiness at school (because of noise in narrow hallways), insomnia (because of house sounds), and misery at family meals (because of chewing sounds) may all point to an auditory processing problem. A teen's insistence on raggedy clothes and only the finest sheets, along with resistance to new foods and beach trips, may point to inefficient tactile processing. Reluctance to drive, difficulty with schoolwork, and confusion at the mall may indicate visual processing difficulties. A passion for jumping over waterfalls or riding motorcycles may suggest an unusual craving in the vestibular system for action-packed movement sensations.

Behavior means something! When you have a picture of the adolescent's sensory difficulties all through the day, you will be able to make transformative changes in his or her life, as well as in your family circle.

PART I

FOCUSING ON SENSORY PROCESSING DISORDER

CHAPTER 1

Seeking Answers about "Out-of-Sync" Adolescents

Certain boys and girls respond to unremarkable experiences in remarkably unusual ways. They may resist going places and being with other people. They may reject hugs . . . or crave them constantly. They may go, go, go . . . or lack get-up-and-go. They may dress sloppily, eat only pasta, drop and break everything, whimper or rage over "nothing" for no apparent reason, insist on doing things their way, and act immaturely for their age, even as they grow. With their late and slow, or rapid and intense, or otherwise "off" responses, they seem out of sync with other people and the world.

It isn't that these out-of-sync kids *won't* do what others do easily—it is that they *can't*. A likely cause of their bewildering behavior is a neurological difficulty called sensory processing disorder (SPD). SPD occurs in the central nervous system when one's brain can't react typically to sensory messages, coming from one's body and environment, in order to function smoothly in daily life.

I bumped into SPD forty years ago. Learning about it changed my life. In 1976, I started teaching music and movement at St. Columba's Nursery School in Washington, DC. That same year this independent school voluntarily began "mainstreaming" children with developmental challenges.

Teaching children with special needs was new to me. Indeed,

everything about teaching was new to me. Becoming a teacher wasn't my plan. In college I focused on poetry, music, and dance classes and dozed through a basic psychology course about child development that I took only because it met the science requirement and fit my schedule. My dream after graduation was to dance in Broadway chorus lines. Instead, I got married and soon had two delightful, typically developing little boys.

So, starting out as a teacher of children with developmental differences, I was multi-handicapped: no coursework in education, no teaching experience, no family members with special needs, and an ordinary tree-climbing, hopscotching, school-loving girlhood. The only reason I got the job at St. Columba's, the preschool my sons attended, was that the director divined in me a spark of some potential.

I learned fast and loved the job. As I expected, the preschoolers who were developing typically were fun to teach. Unexpectedly, I also clicked with kids who were blind and deaf or who had spina bifida, Down syndrome, one arm, cerebral palsy, and other conditions. These children with identified special needs were responsive and eager to learn. I was eager to learn, too, and when I figured out how to help them play rhythm instruments, enact "Goldilocks," and move through obstacle courses, they were exceedingly fun to teach.

But, oh, the others—a handful of kids who had *unidentified* special needs! Talk about a "handful"! This one, when I strummed the guitar, covered his ears and yelled, "Shut up!" At snack time, that one would eat only pretzels and refused every apple and carrot, saying, "My mother told me never to eat this." This boy yanked off his shirt and wore flip-flops in winter. That boy wore hats and jackets on the warmest days.

This girl crashed into other kids, tables, and trees and never sat when she could sprawl. That girl hardly moved; when she had to, she clung to banisters or her teacher's leg. This one got dizzy standing up; that one was a constant, spinning blur.

This child couldn't find his own cubby or the shiny buttons mingled in the bean table or his own elbow. That one couldn't distinguish between a lullaby and a march. Another child couldn't clap, catch a balloon, climb a ladder, or crouch to touch his knees and toes. This one couldn't spread jam on toast; that one couldn't begin to dig to China.

I wondered about these children who met ordinary experiences with a "fight-flight-fright" response; they became aggressive or they fled or they froze with fear. Clumsy, picky, confused, abrupt, or inappropriate, they were out of sync. They weren't naughty or "bad" kids; they didn't wake up every morning scheming how to infuriate their parents or sabotage their teacher's daily plan. They were wonderful kids when everything was "just right" and could be the funniest, kindest, smartest, dearest, most creative students.

I loved them the best. I tried to help them have fun at school. I wanted to know what was happening in their bodies to make the occupation of childhood so difficult. I wondered what would happen to them as they grew up.

What could I do to help my confused and confusing little students grow up to be in sync with the world? Somebody must have the answers, and I had to find out.

After teaching preschoolers for ten years, one day I heard Lynn Balzer-Martin, PhD, OTR/L, describe sensory processing disorder.

My jaw dropped. Bingo! SPD explained all those perplexing behaviors!

On the spot, I became an avid student of SPD and helped Lynn screen one thousand preschoolers for signs of SPD. Learning about the disorder became my passion; teaching parents and teachers about it became my mission.

Since my first book about SPD, *The Out-of-Sync Child*, was

published in 1998, parents have asked me, "Will my child grow out of it?" Whether they are certain or just have a hunch that their children have SPD, parents yearn to hear that their children will not struggle forever with sensory experiences and will develop well enough to function smoothly in daily life. Parents constantly worry and wonder:

- Will my child have a meaningful and gratifying life?
- Will he use his beautiful mind—and flourish in school?
- Will she ever eat like other people?
- Will I ever be able to hug and kiss him?
- Will he learn to make conversation?
- Will she develop close friendships? Will she be invited to parties, and will she want to go? Will she date and discover romance?
- Will he play active games and sports?
- Will she learn to manage noisy, odorous, crowded places, such as the cafeteria, dormitory, mall, or Disney World? Will she ever like walking on the beach?
- Will he learn to handle going to the doctor and sitting in the dentist's chair?
- Will she eventually care about how she looks or smells? Will she willingly brush her hair and take a shower?
- Do difficulties improve, or worsen, or follow some predictable pattern?
- Does everything turn out all right in the end?

I yearn, in turn, to give an answer more satisfying than "It all depends . . . I really don't know." Indeed, nobody knows.

Every person—with or without SPD—is unique. As children

grow, numerous factors influence their development, such as their level of sensory dysfunction, the age when SPD was diagnosed and therapy began, the types of treatment, co-occurring conditions, temperament and self-awareness, family members' and teachers' involvement, home and school environments, and more.

Another reason that nobody knows is that researchers do not yet have the funding to follow a cohort of children from infancy to adulthood in a longitudinal study that would help to predict how individuals with SPD turn out. One thing is for sure: research that has been done shows clearly that the more family support children receive, the better outcomes they will have.

I don't know how teens with SPD turn out because my expertise is with young children. And I don't know because I don't have sensory issues. (Well, *maybe just a little oversensitivity*, when my hands are touching sticky finger paints or bread dough.)

Thus, I have gathered stories from the true authorities. These are adolescents and adults who teach us how it feels to cope with SPD because *they are living with it.*

Some writers were preschoolers when their parents reached out for support. Some are young speakers and attendees whom I met at workshops and conferences. Others heard about the book project from bloggers in the growing SPD community on the Internet, or from their occupational therapists. Some adult contributors are parents. Others are professionals—several of whom grew up with SPD themselves—who work with tweens and teens.

I asked contributors to write about aspects of life with SPD that they wanted other people to hear and understand. I encouraged them to describe memorable experiences of "seeking sync"—i.e., their successful or not so successful attempts, say, to play basketball or go on a date. They welcomed the opportunity. For years, most of them have felt disbelieved, disrespected, and ignored. Until now, few have felt comfortable talking about sensory issues.

I asked everyone to write from the heart, and they sure did! The stories poured in. They are vibrant, poignant, funny, determined, angry, resigned, satisfied, grateful, gracious—the full gamut. You will find many contributors agreeing that the hard work involved in managing SPD has made their lives and their relationships more precious than anyone could have predicted.

For example, Shonda Lucas tells an amazing story. When Shonda was growing up, everybody wondered about her quirky behavior, but nobody understood that SPD was the cause. Overwhelmed, oversensitive, never still, and ever clumsy, she stumbled through adolescence. Fortunately, Shonda learned to make changes, develop her strengths, and transform her life.

Here, she tells us how she evolved from a confused girl into a confident woman. A story like hers could be the story of the adolescent in your life.

DANCING TO MY OWN QUIRKY BEAT
SHONDA LUCAS

"She's just quirky."
   "She's spirited."
   "She's picky."
   "She's clumsy."
   "She's scatterbrained."
   And of course . . . "She'll grow out of it."
   These were phrases I heard my entire childhood, especially to justify why I did some odd things. My teachers and family had no idea what sensory processing disorder was. They thought I just danced to the beat of my own drum.
   Usually, everything bothered me. I felt bombarded by sensations. Other times, I didn't notice them at all and would slump over and sleep.

I had a hard time transitioning between activities, usually requiring relocation and refocusing by my mom. I had more than my share of bumps and bruises as I was very clumsy and would misstep and trip over nothing.

I was eleven when I finally learned to ride a bike because of my balance issues, and eighteen when I learned to drive because I had trouble with space and where the car was on the road and especially with parking.

I often picked things up with more force than necessary. One time I was helping my grandmother with laundry and picked up a detergent bottle. It wasn't as heavy as I expected and I threw it across the laundry room, over my shoulder! She thought I was being a smart-ass and did it on purpose...but I wasn't. I remember feeling, "Wow, I'm really strong," only to realize, no, I had just misjudged...again.

I've always had a bad way with button-ups. I have to start at the bottom to make sure I get the buttons lined up correctly. Lining up zippers isn't easy. And belt loops? Always miss at least one!

Cursive was a curse! I hated handwritten assignments because my writing was horrible and would get worse the more I had to write.

I would slump my shoulders. My grandmother swore it was to "hide my endowments," but I have a weak core. Sitting up still takes a lot of energy. She would make me walk with books on my head to straighten my posture.

I was notoriously messy. My room looked like a tornado ran through it, my hair was forever tangled because I didn't want it brushed, and I loved to play in the dirt. I was a tomboy, climbing, jumping, and keeping up with the neighborhood boys. I preferred jeans and soft T-shirts to lace and craved physical contact. Be it hugging, wrestling, fighting, or a spanking, I thrived on it, and it often got me in trouble.

I was partial to hanging upside down on the playground bars or on my closet rod (which fell down a time or two with me on it). I was upside down anywhere I found a way to be inverted. Tire swings and merry-go-rounds were awesome fun. I also liked to swim in the sandbox; yes, I said *swim* in the sandbox from one side to the other. My peers thought I was a little odd but most of them accepted me anyhow, thankfully.

I usually had my hair in a short bowl cut because when it was longer, I had a bad habit of chewing on it. I chewed shirt ties, pencil erasers, foam cups, and paper—anything I could get my teeth on, really.

I had a very limited diet; I wasn't able to handle certain smells and textures, like lima beans, which just feel funny. Added to those aversions were food allergies, and that meant I had seriously limited culinary experiences growing up.

As I got older in high school and college I was told I had ADHD and was possibly bipolar because at times it was virtually impossible to sit still. I would feel almost wild inside. Studying was difficult and lecture courses were especially excruciating. Being in a huge lecture hall where sounds bounced, fluorescent lights buzzed, and other students were whispering amongst themselves was a nightmare.

I had a hard time engaging in activities most teens enjoy. Crowds were (still are) my enemy. I was totally overwhelmed by them visually, plus having people in my space was like an all-encompassing torture. I couldn't focus or think with all the separate conversations happening or the different colognes and perfumes swirling around. Basketball games drove me crazy, because of the way the ball bouncing sounded. Its echo on the gym floor made my skin crawl. Football games, concerts, and parties made me hypervigilant, and that was no fun. My friends thought I was just quirky or anxious.

However, I discovered that when you set me to music I wasn't the clumsy, wild, flighty girl everyone knew. On the dance floor I was graceful and focused and put my energy to good use. I was a quick learner and not shy, making me an obvious choice for center stage. I won several blue ribbons from a national association, was included in Who's Who in American High School Students, and even got my varsity letter in dance. On the dance floor I was no longer quirky, I was finally "normal."

Sadly, I wasn't able to dance my way through life forever. Years passed and I plodded toward adulthood, chewing on pens, sleeping under heavy blankets even in summer, having bouts of energy to the point I thought my heart would explode, shying away from events with too many people. I had trouble holding relationships and friendships together because of my "inverted" ways.

Then I became a foster parent!

I heard about SPD from a fostering peer, and it clicked! I found *me* in a checklist of symptoms; it all made sense now—why I was quirky, why I hated being in certain situations, why I didn't like the feel of lima beans. I no longer felt like something was wrong with me. I started learning about how to control my bouts of SPD, to overcome some of my issues, and to help myself.

This all made such a difference when I was blessed with my son whom I eventually adopted. Although not biologically mine, he was meant to be with me, as he suffers from severe SPD himself. Understanding the disorder personally has helped me sense why he does things that make him ... quirky!

I still have my quirks. I still despise crowded places. I still use chew toys to help me center myself when I get overstimulated. I still don't eat like an adult should, but I'm learning to *try* new foods—although most often, once is enough!

Most importantly, I've learned it is okay to be quirky, spirited, unique—and to dance to the beat of your own drum. The world is full of quirky people, and I'm proud to be one of them! Without my sensory processing disorder, I wouldn't be ... well, *me*.

Shonda grew up and today is active on inclusion and disabilities boards, speaks about special education at the University of Kentucky and in the special needs community, and advocates for adoptive parents of children with SPD and other developmental issues.

How did she develop into a grounded adult after her "inverted" youth?

Along the way she gained the ability to make personal choices that she couldn't have made as a young girl. She learned to decide what is best to meet her needs—to go out or stay home, to try new foods, to gnaw appropriate chewy toys instead of her hair, and so forth. She decided to adopt her foster son, to learn all she could about their common sensory challenges, and to speak out about SPD. Making choices is a wonderful perquisite of maturing.

And as she grew, something else happened, something transformative. She developed what I call "extrasensory grace." I coined this expression, after becoming acquainted with Shonda and other story writers, to name the intrinsic, elegant, spirited, especially gifted talent or quality that comes from within. Extrasensory grace arrives when individuals with SPD learn to love their quirky selves and discover what they are meant to do and do well.

Rachel S. Schneider, an SPD advocate who was diagnosed in her twenties, says, "I think some of that extrasensory grace, at least for delayed-diagnosis sensory adults, is learning to love the you that *you* were assigned, wiring and all. (I wonder if this applies to kids and teens, too, who received earlier treatment.) We need to reach the point where we can say, 'Yes, X challenges me. Yes, I'm not strong in Y. But I am just incredible at Z.' We have to love ourselves somehow, somewhere."

As an adolescent, Shonda radiated extrasensory grace when she was set to music. She wasn't merely the dancer; she was the dance. As an adult, she uses that special quality to reach out to other families with developmental differences, to help them cope, and to bring them peace. What a story!

As you read, you will see that the story writers consider—but can't fully answer—the questions that parents and teens commonly ask. How things are playing out for our writers may be different from how things will play out at your house. Although no one can make certain predictions, I assure you that things can improve.

Here is an encouraging answer to the question, "When does this get better?" It comes from an adult who grew up with SPD and lives with it still; has four teenagers with SPD; and teaches teenagers with SPD. In every sense, she knows about SPD.

IT DOES GET BETTER
LISA WUNDERLICH TAYLOR

"When does this get better?"

I am face-to-face with a teary student who is exasperated by her sensory challenges. She searches my face for an answer.

I smile with empathy, as I remember wondering the same thing at her age. "Well, I can only tell you what it has been like for me. Sensory processing changes as you get older; that much you can count on. The sensitivities, the triggers, and your responses change. As you get older, you'll be more aware and in tune with your body. Does it get better? It's all how you look at it. I say, yes, because I have learned to control how I respond to sensory challenges."

She smiles and goes back to class.

It definitely gets better, even if it doesn't go away completely. As an adult, I know my limitations—and leave the mall, for example, if it's putting me over the edge. I tolerate irritants, like having my teeth cleaned, because I know they will go away.

The biggest difference in being an out-of-sync child versus an out-of-sync adult is how I respond. Of course there are times when I'm overwhelmed by life, like any other person, and with my already hard-wired system, my responses are aggravated. My reaction to a particular sensation is the same as it was in childhood, but the response to the world around me is different. A good balance of what I know is soothing generally keeps me there ... seeking to be "in sync."

So you may wonder what my strategy is for seeking—and finding—sync. If I encounter something that challenges me, I can either figure out a way to deal with it or get out of the situation. Often I must simply be still—find a place—find my inner sanctuary.

The more awareness we develop to accurately label sensations being experienced, the less defensive and resigned we are. For example, I might say, "Right now, I cannot filter the noise outside, so I need to shut the door." This metacognitive approach is also helpful when working with anyone else who is dealing with SPD.

It does get better by being your own advocate, informing others, being authentic with your feelings, and pushing through when it's challenging. We're wired this way with reason and purpose. Watching my teenage children grow up and witnessing the maturation process unfold has taught me the most about myself.

I choose to give of myself daily. If I can impart anything from my own journey that may help others see the gift in the chaos, the extra effort is worth it. Realizing the gifts that SPD can offer ultimately brings organization to a life that otherwise might seem out of control.

Throughout this book, you will hear many voices. Along with advice from professionals whose work focuses on sensory processing issues, and along with my own observations about human development, you will read what people like Shonda and Lisa tell us— sometimes in pain, sometimes in contentment and joy. Taken together, the book's contributors may help you grapple with and overcome the challenges of living with SPD.

CHAPTER 2

Primer: Facts about Typical Development and Sensory Processing Disorder

Knowing basic facts about SPD, perceptual-motor skills, and human development is important for understanding adolescents' out-of-sync behavior. You may be familiar already with these facts if your son or daughter has SPD, or you have SPD, or you treat individuals with SPD. Or you may be familiar with SPD if you have read my book *The Out-of-Sync Child*, first published in 1998 and thoroughly revised and updated in 2005, Lucy Jane Miller's *Sensational Kids* (2014), or Lindsey Biel and Nancy Peske's *Raising a Sensory Smart Child* (2009). Refer to this chapter when you want a quick review. Otherwise, skip it!

If, however, you are a "newbie" and unfamiliar with SPD, please read this primer carefully. It will help you make sense both of the writers' stories and of your teenager's responses to everyday experiences.

TYPICAL DEVELOPMENT
Sensory Processing: When the Senses Are "In Sync"

Sensory processing, also known as sensory integration, is the neurological process of organizing information about sensations that we get from our body and environment to use in daily life. In the mid-twentieth century, the brilliant occupational therapist A. Jean Ayres, PhD, formulated the theory of sensory integration and its impact on human development, learning, and behavior.

Most of us use sensations every second, all day, without a thought. Stairs to climb, apples to chew, friends to hug? Using our senses, we "just do it."

For most of us, sensory processing occurs automatically and effortlessly in our central nervous system (CNS). The brain, at the top of the CNS, receives messages through sensory receptors in the eyes, skin, nose, etc., and quickly reacts to this *sensory input*, telling the body whether and how to respond with *motor* or *behavioral output*.

The result is an ever-flowing, incoming-and-outgoing, sensory-motor dance.

SENSORY INPUT:

- Reception—receiving sensory messages through specific receptors
- Detection—noticing in the CNS that sensations have arrived
- Integration—connecting messages among various sensory systems
- Modulation—regulating and organizing the degree, intensity, and nature of sensory input
- Discrimination—differentiating among and between sensory stimuli

MOTOR OUTPUT:

- Postural responses—moving or stabilizing the body as needed

- Praxis (Greek for "action," "doing," or "practice")—interacting successfully with the environment through three steps:
  - First, conceiving of a complex sequence of unfamiliar actions (*ideation*).
  - Then, doing the necessary *planning and sequencing.* This planning is often called motor planning, which is figuring out how to move your body through a series of new dance steps. (The term "motor planning" is sometimes used interchangeably with praxis.) Planning can also be mental planning, such as deciding the steps you'll take to choose, research, and begin writing about a history topic.
  - Finally, carrying out your plan (*execution*).

Praxis denotes voluntary, coordinated, achievable action. An example is ideating about getting to your homeroom on the first day of high school, planning how to move your body upstairs and through corridors, and executing your motor plan to arrive at your destination. Praxis is about taking the test for your driver's license, about shaving or applying eyeliner the first time, about your first kiss. These multistep activities require abilities that develop gradually, with much practice. A baby couldn't do it.

Sensory processing, of course, is about senses. The senses serve these essential functions:

- Defensiveness, or self-protection, for survival
- Discrimination, for learning
- Action, for participating in daily life
- Satisfaction, for feeling good

Picture yourself about to cross the street. Suddenly your senses
of sight and sound warn you, "Danger!" Self-defensively, without
thinking, without knowing what scares you, you jump back. Whew!
You will survive! Now you can discriminate what the threat was.
Aha! It was just a big, clanking truck. Calmer now, you get moving.
You step off the curb, walk across the street, and go about your
business. Thank you, senses!

Eight Senses

We have eight senses. Five are familiar: touch, sight, sound, smell,
and taste. Three others, less familiar, are the senses of movement,
body position, and internal organs. Dr. Ayres considered the senses
of touch (*tactile*), movement (*vestibular*), and body position (*proprioceptive*) to be the foundation of healthy human development.[1]

The tactile sense (touch) provides our nervous system with information about touching and being touched. We receive tactile
messages through receptors all over the body. The tactile sense
connects us to the world and enables us to:

- Touch people, food, objects, etc., and discriminate
  what we touch
- Be touched without discomfort, and discriminate what
  is touching us on the skin, on the hair, and in the mouth
- Feel heat and cold
- Feel pain
- Feel safe

---

1   Dr. Lucy Jane Miller says, "Unfortunately, in today's world, tactile, proprioceptive,
and vestibular opportunities have been left behind. In their place are computers, iPods,
MP3s, smartphones, etc. Do not give in to these solely visual-auditory devices! Use them to
enrich your world, not replace it."

The vestibular sense (movement) is about gravity. Gravity tries to pull us down, and our day job is to defy it. This sense tells us where our head is in relation to the surface of the earth, how our body moves through space, and if we're balancing. Vestibular messages, received in the inner ear, enable us to:

- Stand erect and sit up straight
- Discriminate that we are upright, lying down, upside down, or falling
- Change our head position without getting dizzy or falling over, as when shampooing in the shower
- Move through space from one place to another, such as across the street
- Be moved unexpectedly and quickly regain our equilibrium, such as being jostled in a crowded school hallway

The vestibular sense has another important job: getting all the other sensory systems to work together to keep us calm and alert. This is the "master sense," helping us develop self-regulation of our arousal level so we can adapt to the ups and downs of daily life. Self-regulation enables us to:

- Wake up ready to go in the morning
- Eat and eliminate
- Cope with changing routines and transitions
- Stay alert at school or work
- Develop conscious self-control to manage anger, excitement, cravings, etc.
- Self-calm when hurt, stressed, or upset
- Fall asleep and stay asleep

The proprioceptive sense (body position) provides information about where our body parts are, how they bend and stretch, and how much force or pressure we use. Proprioceptive sensations come through our muscles and joints. With good proprioception, we can:

- Flex and extend our joints and orient our limbs with sufficient "oomph"
- Exert the "just-right" pressure on people and objects that we contact physically, as when we shake hands or press the gas pedal
- Discriminate where our body is and how fast our body parts are moving

The visual sense (sight) provides information about what we see in the environment. Sensations come through the eyes. The visual sense includes *eyesight* (visual acuity), telling us that we see something, and *visual processing*, telling us what that thing means. For example, eyesight tells us that we see black lines on the chart; visual processing discriminates that the lines denote the letter *E*. The visual sense makes it possible to:

- Use both eyes together (binocularity) for merging two separate images into one, e.g., to see one moon in the sky
- Detect:
  - Movement, such as an approaching person or a fluttering curtain
  - Line, such as the horizon or the edge of the stage
  - Contrast, such as sunlight versus shadow
- Visually analyze and discriminate differences and likenesses, such as finding a book on the library shelf or a friend in the cafeteria

- Perceive the world in 3-D, understanding our position in space relative to people and objects in the environment

The auditory sense (sound) provides information about what we hear in the environment. Sensations come through the outer ears. Auditory acuity tells us that we hear; auditory processing interprets what we hear. This enables us to:

- Hear sounds and localize what direction they are coming from
- Alert to and tolerate loud, unexpected sounds, such as shouts and thunder
- Follow moving sounds, such as footsteps
- Discriminate sounds, such as different voices and cell phone rings, or the teacher speaking in a noisy classroom

The olfactory sense (smell) provides information about scents, through the nose. Olfaction makes it possible to:

- Smell food, people, objects, and environments
- Discriminate which smells are benign, such as flowers and a beloved's scent, and which smells are threatening, such as a gas leak or rancid food

The gustatory sense (taste) provides information about flavors, through the mouth. Gustation enables us to:

- Taste sweet, sour, bitter, salty, and savory food
- Discriminate what is edible and what is not, such as sour milk

The interoceptive sense (internal organs) provides information about sensations coming from inside our bodies. Interoception makes it possible to:

- Be aware of heart rate, breathing, hunger, thirst, and the need to urinate or defecate
- Digest food
- Sweat

As we grow and develop, so do our sensory processing capabilities—our "sense-abilities." Sensory processing starts the progression from what an infant can do to what a young adult is expected to do. Hands-on, concrete, sensory-motor experiences are the foundation of perceptual-motor skills, which are necessary for doing everyday tasks in a three-dimensional world.

Perceptual-Motor Skills

Balance, a function of the integrated vestibular, proprioceptive, and visual senses, makes these everyday activities possible:

- Staying seated and standing in one spot, even when jostled (static balance)
- Going up and down stairs, walking on unstable surfaces, such as sand or gravel, and running (*dynamic* balance)

Bilateral coordination is the ability to move both sides of the body simultaneously. A function of the vestibular and proprioceptive senses, it enables:

- Clapping
- Catching a beach ball

- Carrying a cafeteria tray
- Pumping air into a bicycle tire and pushing a shopping cart
- Reading with both eyes

Body awareness is the mental picture of where your body parts are and how they move and interact. Tactile, vestibular, and proprioceptive sensations are the foundation. Some activities requiring this skill are:

- Getting dressed, brushing teeth, and slinging on a backpack
- Settling into a desk chair or a restaurant booth
- Participating in PE, playing sports, and learning new dance steps

Directionality, a function of the vestibular and proprioceptive senses, is the awareness of up, down, forward, backward, sideways, diagonally, and around. Some activities requiring directionality are:

- Reading maps or instructions for assembling a bookcase
- Parallel parking
- Finding your way back to the car in a multilevel garage at the shopping mall
- Navigating from one classroom to another

Fine motor control, a function of the tactile, proprioceptive, and vestibular senses, is the skill of moving small muscles for precise tasks. Fine motor tasks involve:

- Hands and fingers for manipulating objects—coins, scissors, three-ring binders, needles, doorknobs, keys, forks and knives, hammers and nails
- Eyes to follow moving objects, focus on unmoving objects, and shift your gaze from a far point to a near point, such as copying notes from the board
- Lips and mouth to chew, articulate speech sounds, suck through a straw, and blow through a trumpet

Gross motor control, a function of the tactile, proprioceptive, vestibular and sometimes visual senses, is the skill of moving the large muscles in the arms, legs, and trunk. Activities requiring gross motor control include:

- Running, squatting, jumping, climbing, hiking, and bicycling
- Donning and doffing a sweater and stepping into pants
- Doing heavy work with resistant objects, such as pushing furniture around, pulling a trash can, lifting and carrying a bucket of paint

Laterality, a function of the vestibular and proprioceptive senses, is the ability to move either side of the body separately from the other. This skill enables the left and right hands or feet to make entirely different motions, including:

- Zipping, buttoning, blow-drying hair with a brush
- Opening a jar, spreading peanut butter on bread
- Sharpening a pencil, stabilizing a paper while writing or cutting
- Starting the lawn mower

- Stamping mud off boots, kicking a ball, playing tennis, dancing the Macarena

Midline crossing, a function of the vestibular and proprioceptive senses, is the ability to use one hand, foot, or eye across the imaginary line dividing the two sides of your body. Activities that require crossing the midline include:

- Stirring cookie batter
- Scratching your elbow
- Brushing your hair, putting on earrings

Motor planning, a piece of praxis, is the ability to organize and sequence the steps of an unfamiliar and complex body movement. The proprioceptive, tactile, and vestibular senses are the foundation. Activities that require motor planning include:

- Taking a shower
- Opening and closing an umbrella
- Tossing a salad
- Typing or playing music on a keyboard
- Learning to ride a bicycle or to roller skate
- Getting in and out of the backseat of a car

Visual-spatial awareness, based on the tactile, vestibular, and visual senses, is the understanding of where you are and how to move around in the environment. Daily-life activities requiring this skill include:

- Moving through a crowded corridor or mall
- Backing out of the driveway, steering through traffic, and parallel parking

- Estimating what jar to fit leftovers into
- Visualizing what cannot be seen, e.g., the stairs under-
  foot while carrying a laundry basket, or an art project
  in your mind's eye
- Doing neat paperwork

Auditory-language skills, based on the auditory sense, enable a
person not just to hear sounds and words but to understand and
respond to them. Activities dependent on good auditory-language
skills include:

- Listening to the teacher, remembering and following
  directions
- Articulating speech sounds clearly enough to be un-
  derstood
- Engaging in conversations, answering questions, and
  making apt comments
- Using language for verbal and written self-expression
- Using auditory feedback to self-monitor voice volume

PHYSICAL, INTELLECTUAL, SOCIAL, AND EMOTIONAL DEVELOPMENT–EVERY TEENAGER'S OCCUPATION

Usually, while sensory and motor skills are developing, so are the
body, mind, and spirit. Physical, intellectual, social, and emotional
growth prepares the adolescent for adulthood. This developmental
process is the "occupation" (or perhaps the preoccupation!) of every teenager. Generally, the process goes like this for typically developing tweens, teens, and young adults.

(Please note that this is an overview of the average progression
from childhood to early adulthood. The range of typical develop-

ment is vast. Many healthy children, with or without SPD, deviate from nature's "blueprint" in one or more areas.)[2]

Early Adolescence

Around the ages of nine to twelve, tweens enter puberty. Physically, girls and boys have a growth spurt, usually with hands and feet growing first. Hair grows in armpits and the pubic area. Girls' breasts start to develop, their body shape becomes more curvy, and menstruation begins. Boys' voices deepen, their genitals enlarge, and they start growing facial hair.

In terms of brain development, a neurological process called "pruning" deletes unused synaptic connections and prepares the brain for improved cognitive abilities and logical reasoning. English-speaking children, for example, do not need to roll their r's when they talk, so connections needed for that skill will be pruned, while Spanish-speaking children's connections will be constantly reinforced. Without a purpose and without experiences to strengthen them, neurons weaken and die. Use it or lose it!

Meanwhile, myelination increases in the brain. (Myelin is a substance that wraps a sheath around neurons to strengthen their connections.) This process helps to transmit information more efficiently between brain regions, such as the limbic system and the prefrontal cortex. (In brief, the limbic system deals with emotions and memories. The prefrontal cortex—where feelings, thoughts, and actions come together—enables self-regulation, clear thinking, problem solving, communication, executive decisions, and praxis.)

Occupational therapists often say, "Nerves that wire together,

---

2   With thanks to Laurence Steinberg, PhD, Deborah Shulman, MSW, LICSW, and Jennifer Pleasure, PsyD, for their wisdom and counsel.

fire together," meaning that the more often an action occurs, the easier it becomes. Thus, the more a tween, or anyone, rehearses a thought, e.g., "I can do this," or practices an action, e.g., kicking a soccer ball, the more effective the thought or action becomes.

In terms of intellectual development, increasingly complex brain processes occur. Tweens still tend toward black-and-white thinking and in concrete terms, but more neural connections and life experiences help their reasoning skills to mature.

Socially, adolescents spend more time with their friends and less time with their family.

Emotionally, because of hormones, they begin to behave like yo-yos. Interactions with siblings may shift, often with siblings moving apart from one another.

Midadolescence

In midadolescence, around ages thirteen to eighteen, physical growth continues. Bodies become fuller, taller, and stronger—close to their adult height and weight. Girls ovulate and produce estrogen; boys produce semen and testosterone. They are fertile now and are capable of having babies. Both girls and boys may produce noticeable body odor and pimples.

After puberty, adolescents' internal clock shifts by about two hours. Falling asleep is easier at 11:30 p.m. than at 9:30 p.m.; awakening happens closer to 8:30 a.m. than 6:30 a.m. Sleep deprivation affects behavior, learning, mood, and alertness needed for quick judgment and driving.

As their brains develop, an increase in neurological activity involving dopamine occurs. Dopamine is related to experiencing pleasure and to sensory-seeking behavior. Especially when they are with peers, midadolescents may indulge in high-risk and impulsive behavior—driving fast, drinking, smoking, having sex, and so forth—because their brains have heightened sensitivity to the anticipation of rewards.

Intellectually, their thinking becomes more abstract. They get much better at problem solving. They are more open to listening to others' different points of view.

Socially, teens become more self-conscious about how they look and behave. They may want to conform to the ways that other kids their age dress, drive, and behave. They may turn toward their peers for advice and company and turn away from their parents if they feel that "parents just don't understand." Independence is the name of their game. Especially today, when social networking is such a big part of how adolescents communicate, parents are often left in the dark about their teens' thoughts, worries, and activities.

Emotionally, as sex hormones surge, so do moods. The teenager's hard-to-control emotions usually affect parents and siblings, and it follows that family dynamics may be intense. Siblings at this stage may become closer again, perhaps as allies against their parents.

Late Adolescence and Young Adulthood

Physical growth slows in late adolescence and young adulthood, around ages nineteen to twenty-five. Now young men and women are at their physical peak.

In their brain, pruning slows down. Until about the age of twenty-five, myelination continues to make neural connections more permanent and efficient, especially in the frontal lobe, which is concerned with judgment, self-control, problem solving, and planning ahead. Stronger brain connections lead to better self-regulation (e.g., they can calm themselves before an exam) and self-discipline (e.g., they can "just say no" to risky peer pressure).

Intellectually, their complex cognitive ability strengthens.

They are now more able to plan ahead efficiently, evaluate risks and rewards, solve complicated problems, delay gratification, make mature decisions, control their physical actions, and understand that other people may think and behave differently.

Socially, they seek affiliation with like-minded people. They look for meaningful work and get ready to take on adult roles.

Emotionally, they have more self-control to curb their impulses, tolerate frustration, and be resilient when things go wrong. They may long for intimacy, romance, and permanence with a loving partner.

For all children, with or without special needs, growing up is a demanding process. For tweens and teens with sensory processing disorder, using their senses effectively in daily activities, fine-tuning their perceptual-motor skills, and going through puberty will be even more challenging, as we'll see in the next section.

ATYPICAL DEVELOPMENT
Sensory Processing Disorder (SPD): When the Senses Are "Out of Sync"

Everyone processes sensations. Some people, like those with SPD, do it less efficiently than others. Because of sensory processing disorder (sometimes called "sensory integration dysfunction"), their central nervous system mismanages bodily and environmental sensations. People with SPD have difficulty responding in an adaptive way to sensations that others hardly notice or easily take in stride.

What is life like when sensory systems don't work well? Daily functioning is possible, but for people who struggle to learn, participate, or feel good in their daily doings, life can be frustrating, lonely, and even painful.

How does it feel when one's behavior is misunderstood? To doctors, therapists, and other professionals, SPD can sometimes look like other conditions, such as eating disorders, anxiety, ADHD, bipolar disorder, and obsessive-compulsive disorder (OCD). Thus, SPD is frequently misdiagnosed and treated with medication or therapies that do not address the underlying sensory issues.

"What really helps people understand overresponsive sensory problems," says Dr. Temple Grandin, the well-known autism advocate, "is asking them to imagine extreme examples of what it feels like. Imagine wearing scratchy sandpaper clothes that make you itch all over, all day. Imagine washing your face in a bucket of perfume. Imagine feeling as if you're going to fall off a cliff when you walk a few steps. Imagine sitting right near the stage, next to a rock band's amplifier."

Being deluged by these sensations is to be expected once in a while—but all day, every day? Yes, that is what SPD may feel like.

A study of a large group of general education children found that 16.5 percent have sensory overresponsivity by the age of eight (Ben-Sasson, Carter, and Briggs-Gowan 2009). The prevalence for all types of SPD is rising. If the disorder is unrecognized and untreated, many of these children develop into adults with SPD. Occupational therapists who specialize in sensory issues are dedicated to identifying and treating children as young as possible. The goal is to help all children and adults learn to manage their sensory challenges so they can lead satisfying, productive lives.

In this classification proposed by occupational therapists Lucy Jane Miller, PhD, Marie E. Anzalone, ScD, Shelly J. Lane, PhD, Sharon A. Cermak, EdD, and Elizabeth T. Osten (2007), sensory processing disorder has three primary categories, each with several subtypes.

CATEGORIES AND SUBTYPES OF SENSORY PROCESSING DISORDER (SPD)		
Sensory Modulation Disorder	Sensory Discrimination Disorder	Sensory-Based Motor Disorder
Sensory Over-responsivity	Tactile (Touch)	Postural Disorder
Sensory Under-responsivity	Vestibular (Movement and Balance)	Dyspraxia
Sensory Craving	Proprioceptive (Body Position)	
	Visual (Sight)	
	Auditory (Sound)	
	Olfactory (Smell)	
	Gustatory (Taste)	
	Interoceptive (Internal Organs)	

Here are descriptions of SPD categories and subtypes, with examples to help you connect the dots between terminology and life experience.

Sensory Modulation Disorder

• Difficulty with regulating and organizing the degree, intensity, and nature of responses to sensory input in a graded and adaptive way. Sensory modulation disorder has three subtypes: overresponsivity, underresponsivity, and craving. Also, fluctuating between being overresponsive to some sensations, such as unexpected touch, while craving or being underresponsive to other sensations, such as movement, is common. Sensory fluctuation may be caused by the time of day, environment, fatigue, stress, and other factors.

SUBTYPES OF SENSORY MODULATION DISORDER

• **Sensory Overresponsivity**—Causing the person who is a "sensory avoider" to shrink from stimuli. Not only garish, malodorous, raucous, spicy, jolting, and prickly stimuli, but also mild everyday stimuli can quickly make the sensory avoider irritated . . . very irritated . . . or angry and thoroughly miserable. Overresponsivity is sometimes referred to as "defensiveness."

  • **Tactile:** Light, unexpected touch bothers Emma. She can't bear to have her hair brushed and won't wear a hat. She wears well-worn, long-sleeved, ankle-length clothes to avoid the feeling of air on her skin. She eats soft, mushy food. Being kissed or caressed makes her uncomfortable.

  • **Vestibular:** Aiden gets carsick unless he is the driver. Rocking chairs, elevators, airplanes, and boats also make him uncomfortable. Sometimes he experiences "gravitational insecurity," which is extreme fear and anxiety that he will fall when his head position changes or when he moves through space, as when bending over to tie his shoes, turning his body around, scaling a ladder, or riding in a car.

  • **Visual:** Logan is highly irritated in milling crowds. Strobe lights and flickering fluorescent lights bother him.

  • **Auditory:** In lecture halls, Hannah is annoyed by fluorescent lights buzzing and by classmates whispering

and tapping on keyboards. In the cafeteria, the sound
of people chewing and swallowing bothers her. At ball
games and parties, boisterous noises bother her.

- **Olfactory and Gustatory:** Ethan can't tolerate the
  smell of perfumes and body odor, seaweed, mothballs,
  and new-mown grass. He can't tolerate broccoli, ba-
  nanas, or off-brand cornflakes.

- **Sensory Underresponsivity**—Causing the person who is a
"sensory disregarder" to show slow or little or even no reaction
to stimuli. The person may ignore body-centered and environmental stimuli. He may seem lethargic or lazy and need a lot of
coaxing to get off the couch and out the door. The sensory disregarder needs intense sensory input to "get it."
  - **Tactile:** Kathy can walk barefoot in the snow and step
    into extremely hot bathwater without being aware of
    the extreme temperatures. She is unaware when her
    clothes are twisted or her tights are falling down under
    her dress. She doesn't notice (or tend to) her chronic
    acne or cuts and bruises.
  - **Vestibular:** Freddy frequently trips on air. Unaware
    that he is falling, he doesn't thrust out a hand or foot,
    in protective extension, in time to cushion the fall.
  - **Proprioceptive:** Valerie sits in a W position—on the
    floor with her knees close and feet out to the sides for
    extra stability. As she walks, she slaps her feet on the
    pavement for sensory input.
  - **Visual:** Gus doesn't notice the snowball coming his
    way and doesn't duck in time. He responds slowly
    when people gesture or traffic lights change.
  - **Auditory:** At a football game, Enrique doesn't hear
    his friend calling "Yo!" to get his attention.

- **Olfactory and Gustatory:** Susie doesn't detect that the cheese is moldy.

- **Interoceptive:** Jenna doesn't notice when she has eaten too much spicy salsa or that she needs to go to the bathroom.

- **Sensory Craving**—Causing the person who is a "sensory craver" to seek certain sensations longer and more intensely than others. She seems addicted to stimuli. But added sensory input, instead of being satisfying, causes her to become increasingly disorganized and frenetic in search of ever more stimulation.

  - **Tactile:** Sandy constantly reaches out to touch objects and people.

  - **Vestibular:** Steve craves extremely invigorating activities like mountain biking, skateboarding, and downhill skiing. He is in perpetual motion, rocking on his feet when he stands and jiggling in his seat.

  - **Proprioceptive:** Myrna bumps and crashes into everything and everyone in her path. She constantly gnaws fingernails, hair, pencils, and straws. She always has gum, cookies, or chips in her mouth because she needs to chew. She begs for hugs to get deep pressure.

  - **Visual:** Sara can't get enough of watching sliding doors open and close. At a party, she lifts her face to stare directly at the strobe light.

  - **Auditory:** At a concert or party, Burt gets as close to the amplifiers as possible. Music can never be too loud for him.

  - **Olfactory and Gustatory:** When Larry enters a room, he sniffs the air. He sniffs food, objects, and other people. Now a high-schooler, he must control his urge to lick objects and people—but he would if he could.

- **Interoceptive:** Joan eats a whole pizza or a gallon of ice cream, and then some more, to get the sensation of being full.

Sensory Discrimination Disorder

Causing the person who is a "sensory jumbler" to have difficulty discerning differences among sensory messages, such as how things look, sound, feel, weigh, taste, and smell.

SUBTYPES OF SENSORY DISCRIMINATION DISORDER

- **Tactile** (touch): Josie looks disheveled, with messy hair and unkempt clothes. Buttons, zippers and belts confound her. She seems "out of touch" with her hands and feet, as if they are unfamiliar appendages. When someone touches her she can feel it but doesn't know where on her body she has been touched. Touching and holding objects, she has difficulty perceiving their texture, temperature, shape, size, temperature, or density, and she often drops them.

- **Vestibular** (balance and movement): In an elevator, Scott can't tell if the elevator is rising or descending, and he often feels nauseous. Because of poor coordination and balance, he has never learned to ride a bike.

- **Proprioceptive** (body position): Sophia is confused about how much force to exert and often lifts a book with so much force that she sends it flying, or she squeezes too hard when she hugs a friend. She is clumsy positioning her body to get dressed, especially if she can't see what she is doing.

- **Visual** (sight): Manny stands there for a while looking for the pickle jar in the refrigerator or two matching socks in the dresser drawer. Poor depth perception makes sports activities difficult, because he can't easily judge where and how balls, Frisbees, pucks, and other players are moving. Learning to drive, he has difficulty knowing where the car is on the road, where other cars are in relationship to his, and especially how to parallel park.

- **Auditory** (hearing): Mia is confused in large groups when several conversations are going on around her. She often mistakes a loud, friendly voice for an angry voice, or a "No!" for a "Go!" She has difficulty understanding jokes and puns or remembering song lyrics, a teacher's verbal instructions, or what a friend just told her.

- **Olfactory** (smell): Avery can't tell the difference between cocoa and coffee or between a clean T-shirt and the one he wore all day yesterday.

- **Gustatory** (taste): Charlotte can't discriminate when food is too salty or sweet or that she has a bad taste in her mouth and should brush her teeth.

- **Interoceptive** (internal bodily functions): Dick often doesn't realize that he is hungry or that he needs to have a bowel movement.

Sensory-Based Motor Disorder

Difficulty with movement resulting from inefficient sensory processing, especially in the tactile, vestibular, and proprioceptive senses.

SUBTYPES OF SENSORY-BASED MOTOR DISORDER

- **Postural Disorder**—Causing the person who is a "sensory slumper" to have difficulty stabilizing the body while moving or resting in response to the sensory demands of the environment or task. The person may struggle with sensory-based motor functions, such as muscle tone, motor control, balance, bilateral coordination, and crossing the midline.

  - Roberto slumps at the desk and dinner table. His weak muscles, low tone, and poor core strength make it hard to sit and stay upright. He is clumsy using pencils and scissors, walking on gravel, stepping off the curb, reaching for a coffee mug, swimming, kicking a ball, and other tasks that require him to position his body accurately. He would rather stay seated, because movement takes so much energy!

- **Dyspraxia**—Causing the person who is a "sensory fumbler" to have difficulty with:

  - Ideation, i.e., thinking of an idea for a new, multistep action.

    George's friend Don and his older brother Sam pick him up to go to the movies. Riding in the back seat makes George uncomfortable, but he has no choice. With some effort he climbs in, closes the door, and slumps back. Sam waits for a moment and then says, "Seat belt, dude." George sighs. Oh, yeah, seat belt. Right. That, too.

  - Planning and sequencing the necessary motions.

    To put on this unfamiliar seat belt, George must modulate and discriminate messages from five sensory systems: vestibular, to turn his head, as well as to stay calm and alert; visual, to look for the buckle; proprioceptive, to stretch out his arm; tactile, to grasp the buckle, and proprioceptive again, to gradually draw out the belt; and auditory, to click the buckle into place. Using his senses to do all these tasks does not happen automatically, so George has to think each one through.

- Execution, i.e., carrying out the plan of action.

Sweating, George fumbles with the multistep action and eventually secures the seat belt. Ten minutes after the car pulled into his driveway, off the boys go to the movies.

Clumsiness is something we all endure now and then. Most of us falter with unfamiliar actions that have sequential steps. Try to remember the first time you rode a bicycle, went through an obstacle course, flossed your teeth, followed a complex recipe, played Ping-Pong, or dressed up for a date. Initially, everyone bungles a few steps and must redo them a few times, until these novel tasks become routine.

But unfamiliar actions are full of significant stumbling blocks for the sensory fumbler with dyspraxia. Balancing on a bike and flossing teeth may take many, many rehearsals and much, much effort. It's easy to see that SPD could be disheartening in body, mind, and spirit, but all may turn out well, as many stories here prove.

In sum, the red flags of SPD are unusual responses to sensory input. One sense, several senses, or all the senses may cause problems. Different combinations of modulation, discrimination, and sensory-based motor issues may occur in one person. *SPD is not an "all or nothing" condition.* It may be a little of this and a lot of that, and the issues may differ from day to day, from place to place.

Everyone, everywhere, contends with changes and challenges during adolescence. Teenagers and young adults with SPD struggle with a heavier load than their typically developing peers. The job of maturing can be arduous, indeed, when the senses are out of sync. In the following chapters, we'll explore strategies that can help.

CHAPTER 3

Coping and Hoping

Most contributors to this book have learned to cope and feel comfortable talking about how they got to where they are now. Their outlook is optimistic.

Nonetheless, the struggle of growing up with SPD cannot be ignored. While knowledge and treatment *raise* hope, ignorance and misdiagnosis *raze* hope. As we'll see in the stories and insights that follow, understanding, from within and from others, is essential for growth and progress.

DIFFICULT, DEPENDENT, AND HOPELESS? ME?
KYLIE BOAZMAN

After years of struggling to understand myself, I was diagnosed right before I began tenth grade. I began to read everything I could find. This led to an intense depression as I consumed sad stories that described kids with Asperger's and SPD as difficult, dependent, and hopeless. This information wasn't even remotely accurate for the majority of people with autism spectrum disorder (ASD) and SPD, but I applied everything I read to my situation.

Most fifteen-year-olds are at the stage in their intellectual development when they still tend to see the world in terms of black and white, without much gray. In their emotional development, they are particularly self-conscious, because of their changing bodies, because of social awkwardness, and for countless other reasons. SPD adds complications to teenagers' outlooks. It is no surprise that a fifteen-year-old with sensory issues would think, "Someone says X about certain people with my diagnosis, thus X must be true about me, too." (We'll hear more from Kylie in chapter 12, where she describes her experience with occupational therapy.)

Faltering hope is common. Because being in sync with the world and connecting with others is a constant struggle, people with SPD often feel hopelessly lost, unseen, and unknown. They cry, "Here I am! I matter! Sorry to be a klutz, sorry to disappoint you . . . I don't act this way on purpose . . . I can't help it. See me, hear me, appreciate me! Understand me!"

Other emotional issues and negative feelings may also impede adolescent development. Shame is an example. Human beings feel shame when conscious of doing something improper, silly, dishonorable, or hurtful, and this awareness of our behavior makes us feel awful about ourselves. Shame, a primitive affect like fear, triggers an automatic fight-or-flight response, readying us to resist or run when we feel in danger. In *The Ecology of Learning* (2011), Suzanne P. Starseed explains how this response distorts a person's vision, hearing, motor control, attention, memory, and intellectual function. Under great stress, everyone's ability to think clearly, learn, and relate to others is jeopardized. This ability is threatened even more when a person with SPD feels that she is not in control at school or in social settings, for instance, and that she can't succeed although she is trying hard.

Shame may be corrective if we act dishonestly or without compassion when we should "know better." For instance, after first learning about SPD, I was ashamed when I recalled how I had treated several children in my classroom. I had scolded a tactilely overresponsive boy for shoving me away when I approached; it turned out he was just trying to protect himself. I had rebuked a dyspraxic girl who poured salt into the cookie dough; she was just trying to participate in the baking activity. At the time, these children "pressed my buttons," and I didn't know why. To my shame, I had made them cry—and I wanted to run away and hide. Understanding SPD and the reasons for their behavior taught me to know better. I became a better teacher and, I hope, a better person.

What has surprised me is the number of stories from young people with SPD about *their* sense of shame. Many describe feeling ashamed for worrying, frustrating, angering, and perplexing their parents, teachers, and peers. The more out of sync an adolescent feels in his body and environment, the more ashamed he can become. The more ashamed he is, the more out of sync he feels, in a downward spiral. Furthermore, he may feel that he is a bad person for causing so much disruption.

Guilt, like shame, embarrassment, anger, sadness, and rejection, also echoes through many contributors' stories. Most of us feel guilt when conscious of doing something injurious, mean, or wrong, and this awareness makes us feel remorseful about our actions or words that hurt others. Guilt can help us become more mindful of our voluntary behavior.

Many people with SPD, however, often feel guilt for their involuntary behavior, such as being physically clumsy or socially awkward. Inefficient motor coordination and limited conversational skills are not their fault but can make them believe they are doing something—or everything—wrong.

Self-blame also abounds. Teenagers with SPD may feel weak and inadequate. They may wonder, "If other people can tolerate noise, odors, escalators, and wool mittens, if other people can keep calm in stimulating situations, if other people can do this and that, why can't I?"

Coping with negativity is a huge challenge for every adolescent and young adult with SPD. Some teens attempt to cope by turning away from other people and becoming loners. Some smoke, drink alcohol, or take drugs to get high and to lower their anxiety and confusion. They may use addictive substances to dull the sensory pain if they are overresponsive—or to get a rush of sensory stimulation if they are underresponsive or crave sensations.

Some hurt themselves, cutting their arms and legs with little razor slashes or burning themselves with cigarettes or other hot items. The physical and psychological reasons for adolescents' self-injurious behavior are worrisome and complex. Some people with SPD say that feeling something is better than feeling nothing, and that after hurting themselves, they "feel real."

SPD HANDLER

To help a person with SPD calm down and cope with physical discomfort and emotional stress, an excellent technique is providing deep pressure—the kind of intense tactile and proprioceptive input that comes from a big bear hug. Hugging is truly therapeutic. Everyone, with or without SPD, needs a partner, parent, teacher, or friend to provide a hug or two (or twelve) a day. Rachel S. Schneider has come up with the term "SPD handler" to denote just such a person who helps an individual with SPD to interact better with the world by hugging and holding, pressing and squeezing, in the just right way. Rachel notes that having a handler is reciprocal, as a handler sometimes needs special handling and support, too.

Below, three writers address this subject of negative feelings and express their hope that people they encounter will acknowledge what they are going through and help them out.

EMOTIONAL EFFECTS OF SENSORY OVERLOAD
KEVIN LARSON

People need to know that if one thing hurts, it *all* hurts. So if someone with SPD says something's bothering them, take it seriously. If it isn't fixed, it will get worse and worse and worse.

My family can't go to noisy restaurants, we have to follow a semi-predictable schedule, and whenever I get overwhelmed, we all have to leave. I know it's not fair to everybody else, but I can't help myself. It makes me feel as though I've let them down.

The worst thing about having SPD is when I go into sensory overload. It's embarrassing because it's always where other people are. It makes me angry because I lose control of my emotions, and it makes me sad because I end up hanging around with adults when I really want to be able to hang around with other teens. I want them to like to hang around with *me*.

People with autism and sensory issues aren't dumb. Most of us are very smart! We're just like everyone else, except more sensitive to sound, sight, touch, smell, motion . . . to everything in our environment. So if others want to help us, *tone it down* and give us a chance. (Be quiet, slow down, give me a minute!)

NEVER DOUBT MY FEELINGS
CHLOE ROTHSCHILD

If I say I need a minute or two, give me time and do not rush me. Don't punish me for needing a break. I am punished enough by my guilty and overloaded feelings. Listen to me, and never doubt what I tell you or my feelings. Don't laugh them off like they are no big deal, as they are a big deal to me.

When I do start to feel agitated, I know now what to do to help myself feel better again. But I still make mistakes, and I still have my moments. Becoming an expert at self-regulating my own behavior is something that will take years to learn, and with more and more experience in doing it, I am sure it will get easier.

WHAT SHOULD I EVEN BE ASHAMED FOR?
PAUL BALIUS

Growing up, I never talked to anyone about my condition. I did not know how. It just became part of who I was. It did not make sense to me, so how could I bring it up? It became my hidden secret.

Even I find my condition very strange. I know that most will never understand, and some will even make fun of my condition. This has happened as I grew and shared some details about it. It is hurtful when someone mocks something that is so painful to me. However, if being mocked will help a fellow sufferer or help a parent of a child, then so be it. My compassion for others outweighs my pride.

Growing to manhood was difficult. Men of our time are faced with many distorted examples of what being a man means. So many men develop inappropriate ways to prove themselves, to fit in among other men, to be admired by women. In my life, this issue was compounded by low self-esteem caused by the shame of having a sensory condition. It was painful to be around men in most situations. I felt weak, not masculine enough, because I would have pain from normal everyday sights and sounds. I felt unworthy. I could not fit in. I was so lost growing up, trying to become a man in all the wrong ways. Loners are outcasts. How could I ever feel like a man?

I was very wild as a teenager, always trying to run away from something. I found equally wild boys, and we would do crazy things. Several times I stole cars and went on adventures. I was arrested in three different states during some of these adventures. One time I was detained when I was fifteen. Another boy in my cell who seemed crazy sneaked up behind me and started to choke me with a rolled-up towel. I did not try to stop him.

This was a great turning point in my life. I was tired of the pain, the running. I was not afraid to die. This may not be what anyone would want to read, but sometimes hidden pain overwhelms our hope. Looking back I see now that this moment was necessary to become who I am now. It started a whole new life for me. I had to lose hope to discover that there is hope.

But the transition from hopeless to hopeful did not happen overnight. Eventually I learned that I was not alone. I read a book, met people in an online group, and discovered there were others like me. What a wonderful thing it is to know now what sensory input disturbs me and what I can do to remedy the situation. I am sad for all those kids who suffer with sensory issues and cannot correct their situations. I hope someday, like me, they can.

I began to speak of my condition openly to people like me. Oh, what joy! Being able to share my hidden secret is nothing less than amazing! I was literally freed from it. The best part about speaking out is that people generally welcome hearing about my condition. Everyone carries some burden. I believe it helps when a person says he understands burdens and can share theirs, which they may have borne and been ashamed about for so many years.

What I was ashamed of then, I now carry no shame about. What should I even be ashamed for? It is not what I did, but rather how I was made. Why should I be ashamed that I am designed differently? Does a Ford sit in shame because it is not a BMW? Exposing my secret is like coming out of the darkness and basking in the sunlight. It is like being found innocent after claiming your innocence for many years. Justified. Accepted. No longer in hiding.

Many of us spend too much time covering up who we are. Wouldn't it be great to just be you?

I am convinced that in the future there will be a growing understanding and acceptance of people who have sensory challenges. I know these challenges cross several spectrums of disorders, and so I am hopeful that the community will expand and merge with others who can learn and grow.

Going from hopeless to hopeful does not happen overnight. Learning about SPD and becoming more efficient and effective in your daily doings takes time and work. Living a sensory lifestyle and developing problem-solving skills (see chapter 12) can help young people cope with SPD and begin the process of getting in sync.

HELP AND HOPE FOR SPD

Daniel Travis

Since writing this in his early twenties, Dan has become a full-time Web developer and dedicates his own organization, SPD Life (www .spdlife.org), to advocating for adults with SPD.

At twenty, I was depressed, confused, and desperate. I simply couldn't figure myself out. I knew something was wrong and had begun to lose all hope that things would someday get better.

Finally, I found SPD, the answer to all my questions. I found that I wasn't alone, that a large percentage of people have similar problems, and that many are still searching for answers. If you need guidance, as I once did, I offer this five-step "RE" process to help you through one of the roughest, yet most important, periods of your life, the period that comes right after discovery.

1. **REsearch** . . . SPD to see how it has impacted your daily life. Join an online group and study the archives of knowledgeable people. The more you learn, the more you'll understand, and the sooner your questions about yourself will be solved. Trust me, reading everything is worth the time and effort.

2. **REframe** . . . your perspective on your daily actions, decisions, memories, and thoughts. Now that you understand SPD, you will see how your life is formed around it, or even run by it. This revelation can alter your whole outlook, and knowing which of your quirks have a sensory base will allow you to take the blame off yourself and improve your self-image. You will be able to anticipate when sensations or situations may upset you and to navigate through life better.

3. **RElive** . . . the times when sensory issues made your life miserable or even unbearable. You remember being a struggling child, and now the world expects you to be a confident adult. However, you didn't receive the guidance that you so badly needed all these years. You have been hurt, crushed, left out, and defeated. When you needed the most help, people might have ignored you, made negative comments, or called you names. Now you've discovered that you are not to blame!

This is huge! Allow yourself to grieve for your losses, your hardships, your pain, and the times you badly needed an advocate. Vent in online SPD communities, and talk to people who understand and support you. Forgive yourself for the things you did when you really couldn't have done any better to cope, and remove all those harsh and false labels that many have given you, or that you have given yourself.

4. **REward** . . . yourself for all that you have been able to accomplish before you first heard the acronym "SPD." Even if you can't think of much personal success, remember that after all these years of being stuck, on edge, or uncomfortable in your body, you are still here! Without any help, you are a strong survivor, no matter what you or anyone else has thought. Reward yourself for all the things you have attempted to do, and stop being so hard on yourself for your failures. They are not your fault.

5. **REwire** . . . your brain through occupational therapy using a sensory integrative approach (OT-SI). It is never too late to make changes in your sensory systems. Love yourself enough to make this amazing change. Find an OT who is able to treat a teenager or adult.

Going through these five "RE" steps may be hard and may take years, as sensory issues can't just go away through some prescription drug. At times, you may wonder if you can make it. You may find it hopeless, and feel that nobody will ever love and cherish you in the unique way you deserve to be supported. However, change can, and does, come.

Stop listening to those who don't understand you and start believing those who see the wonderful person you are, despite your quirks and behavioral issues. You have a home in the SPD community, where people will support you every step of the way. At last, you have found help and hope. One day you will look back in awe, amazed at the progress you've made and the foundation of a better life.

—Excerpted with permission from an article in *S.I. Focus* magazine (now called *Sensory Focus*), Spring 2009

Faced with sensory obstacles, most adolescents and young adults surely have many moments of feeling overwhelmed and hopeless. Kylie, Kevin, Chloe, Paul, and Dan have "been there, done that." But their unhappy teenage experiences with SPD have not daunted them. Rather, their experiences have filled them with resolve and that extrasensory grace to build a much better life. Their stories give hope.

PART II

COPING WITH DAILY ACTIVITIES

CHAPTER 4

Grooming for the Day Ahead

We all want to inhabit a body that hums along, so we can harmonize with the world around us. We want to be able to arise from bed, put on clothes, go downstairs, eat breakfast, hug somebody, hoist a backpack or briefcase, walk or ride to school or work, and flow through the day, in tune.

Performing these routine tasks depends on efficient tactile, proprioceptive, and vestibular processing. These three sensory systems are the "biggies" that govern how we touch and are touched, how we position and use our body parts, and how we move through space.

Everything we do involves touch, position, and movement. Can you think of an action that does not? Even lolling on the couch, we touch the upholstery, we stretch out or curl up, we blink, we swallow. According to the renowned psychiatrist and authority on child development Stanley I. Greenspan, MD, who treated children with ASD and SPD, "Our great human commonality is touching and being touched, moving and being moved."

When touching and moving are out of sync, then planning and carrying out ordinary activities can be quite a challenge. Hearing about the experiences of young people with SPD, we can appreciate how it feels to be inside their body as they manage to get through an ordinary day.

Start with grooming. Showering, shaving or putting on makeup, trimming fingernails, shampooing and brushing hair, getting haircuts, brushing teeth, and other sprucing-up tasks can be grueling for adolescents with overresponsivity and dyspraxia. Because their *neurological reaction* to sensations is out of sync, their *behavioral response* to these sensations will be out of sync, too.

Getting ready to leave the house may be exhausting. And ahead is the whole day to slog through. No wonder that some adolescents, needing to conserve their energy, would rather give up than clean up.

But during the teenage years, grooming matters immensely. Typical adolescents pay keen attention to the "right" clothes, hairstyles, scent, and so forth. Being in sync with peers is part of the teenager's job description.

Would atypical adolescents also like to be fashionable, fragrant, and in sync? The answer is "It all depends," because people with SPD are, well, atypical.

Some care very much about grooming; they are hyperaware and self-critical about how others view them. They would like to get this grooming routine right but can't do it alone. Awkward social skills often accompany SPD, so they may not know how to ask their peers about personal things like hair products, shaving cream, and acne lotion. Being teenagers, quite possibly they wouldn't dream of consulting their parents.

Other teenagers with SPD do not care much how they look or what others think, but they usually don't try to be offensive—unless being offensive is the only way to be noticed.

HOW NOT TO LOOK LIKE AN UNMADE BED

Bobbi Sheahan

Sensory issues are among the many things that Bobbi Sheahan, her husband, and kids have in common, and about which they keep their sense of humor. A former assistant district attorney, Bobbi is now a full-time mother of three. She has worked as an editor at *Future Horizons*. She is a columnist for *Sensory Focus* magazine and the coauthor of three books, including *What I Wish I'd Known about Raising a Child with Autism*.

It's a paradox: many folks on the autism spectrum and with SPD will notice the slightest imperfection or inconsistency in someone else's appearance or smell, yet they can be oblivious to the fact that they have body odor, have just messed in their pants, or look like an unmade bed.

If you (or a loved one) don't really care that much about fashion and grooming, it's time to learn a new set of skills. So, where do you start? Here are six steps.

1. Find a mentor. Ask a friendly person you know or a relative who actually enjoys fashion and grooming if she would consider going shopping with you. She may be delighted, especially if she already thinks you could use a serious makeover. Tell her your budget and a few items you want. Tell her that since you hate shopping, and she likes it and also has good taste, you'd like her to help you pick something out. Here's one of those social rules that nobody ever tells you: it flatters people when you ask them to help you. Your purchases may reflect more of her style than yours, but that's be-

cause you may have no style. But you will end up with
a cool wardrobe, thanks to her.

2. Keep your clothing clean, with no holes or stains.
None. I'm not just talking about visible stains or holes,
I'm talking about any stains or holes, period. What
you and I may think is visible versus what someone
else sees—well, they ain't the same thing. Leave yourself lots of margin for error. This is a new skill, remember? If you have a favorite cardigan that you've
worn for five winters, trust me when I tell you this: if
it's smelly and dirty, your classmates want you to get a
new one.

3. Smell good. Stay with this step until you have mastered it. This doesn't mean piling perfume or deodorant on an unwashed body. This means, at a minimum,
that you bathe or shower daily, whether you think you
need it or not, and use deodorant. Use it after you
shower or bathe.

    Don't reuse your socks just because they're still
mostly white. We can smell them. And, as for perfume
or cologne, don't trust yourself. Get a mentor for that,
too. Someone who can tell you what smells good on
you and how much is too much.

    While we're talking about smell, you need fresh
breath, as well. A good rule of thumb: If someone offers you a breath mint, take it! They might be trying to
tell you tactfully that you need it.

4. Have good hair. It's easier than it sounds. If it's unusually good or unusually bad, your hair is one of the first

things that people notice. So you don't have to adopt a high-maintenance hairstyle, especially if you're like me and won't maintain it. A good haircut goes a long way. If you really don't want to have to fuss with your hair, find a hairdresser who can give you a low-maintenance style, and have it cut every month. Yes, every month, because the less hair you have, the fewer things can go wrong with it. Don't have it cut extra-short in the hopes of going longer between haircuts. And don't cut your own hair. I tried that in college until a friend offered to cut it because she said that I looked like Elvis.

5. Take care of your nails. Fingernails shouldn't be dirty or ragged, and they should exist.

    If you are a young woman, this is a problem that you can outsource. You can go sit still for an hour while a stranger in a nail salon gives you a manicure or puts on fake nails, which will look awesome for a couple of weeks. This kind of girliness, which makes me look like I do give a rip about how I look, really appeals to me. And toenails—same deal. Even if it's the dead of winter and nobody is going to see your feet, trust me. A pedicure will make you look and feel good.

    If you are a young man, keeping your nails clean and trimmed (with a clipper, not with your teeth) should suffice.

6. Finally, get creative. Want to wear fashionable clothes? Want to have beautiful skin? You now know how to begin going about it. Also, if you have the courage to ask a few friends what they would do if they gave you a

makeover, you may find that you have Mad Scientist eyebrows or visible nose and ear hairs, or (gasp!) that you're being unintentionally immodest. Hearing it once may be embarrassing, but you can fix it, and then you won't have to be embarrassed again.

Why should we care about grooming? Because in our society, poor grooming is career limiting, and it also limits one's social opportunities. Some people with autism and SPD may need help in understanding that grooming skills can be learned like anything else. A memorable moment for Temple Grandin was when her boss gave her deodorant and instructed her to use it. Resentful then, she is grateful now.*

Personal hygiene is really important. Really, really important. Don't be embarrassed that it's a struggle. Temple Grandin is—if you ask me—the smartest person ever, and she had to be told. So, here I am, telling you. I hope that I've convinced you that this is an issue that you can address pretty painlessly.

—Adapted with permission from an article in *Autism Asperger's Digest* (May–June 2014)

* In *Thinking in Pictures*, Temple Grandin writes that her boss, Emil Winnisky, "did me a great favor. With much embarrassment I remember the day that he plunked a jar of deodorant on my desk and told me that my pits stank." This scene is also in the movie *Temple Grandin*.

THEY CALLED ME "COCKROACH"

DANIEL TRAVIS

It was just like any other Monday morning. Soon I would be leaving for school, so I went through my usual morning preparation routine. Not wanting to get out of bed to save my life, I lingered as long as I could before finally getting up and throwing on the same exact outfit I had worn every day for the last week. By the time my brothers were already eating breakfast and preparing to head to school, I was still double-checking everything to make sure my tag-free shirt was on the right way.

I thought of myself as an absentminded professor, and it wasn't uncommon to see me with my shirt on inside out, backward, or both. I put on a pair of socks, sliding them up as far as I could, as I couldn't stand to have them loose or to expose my legs to outside touch. I was a slow and clumsy dresser, but I could do it.

I didn't comb my hair. I didn't brush my teeth. I didn't—wouldn't—take a bath or a shower, neither in the morning nor at night. My T-shirt was loose and dirty, but I didn't care. My shorts were stained and hadn't been changed in a few weeks, but that never deterred me; neither did the fact that I had been wearing the same pair of briefs for the past month.

I looked down at my hands and searched for the openings—the places where I could dig in and peel off more layers of skin. My hands were incredibly dry and flaky, frequently cracking and bleeding. I should have used lotion, but lotion was always too hot and painful for my hands. I could have stopped washing them a hundred times each day, but every time I touched something, someone else, or even my own body sometimes, I simply had to wash them.[1]

I finally made it to the kitchen as my brothers were getting ready

---

1 Because frequent hand washing is a sign of obsessive-compulsive disorder (OCD), people with SPD who do it because of tactile overresponsivity may be misdiagnosed.

for Mom to take them to the private school they attended. Next year I would go there, too. Changing schools would likely mean giving up whatever friendships I had been working on for the past six years in public school. I figured I was okay with that, as I was always low on the totem pole. I had been teased and bullied, so I generally turned to self-harm, as it tended to keep others from attacking me.

Mom and my brothers left. I looked at the clock and sighed deeply. It was late, and I had to leave. The walk to school used to be mildly fun, when I had a companion. He was a boy who lived around the corner, and we had known each other forever. He no longer seemed interested in walking with me, however, so I walked to school alone.

Eventually, I made it into class and sat down at my desk, which was grouped with a few others. I was with three girls and another boy. As I approached my chair, I heard it starting already . . .

"Ewww! He's here again," one of the girls shouted, sliding away from me.

You see, they noticed my poor hygiene: how rarely I bathed, how bad my dandruff was, how I continued to wear the same clothing, and how dry and cracked up my hands were. To them, I was despicable and untouchable.

To them, I was just the nickname they gave me, "Cockroach." I still remember their calling me that every day. I went along with it because, on the one hand, I didn't know what else to do. I fed into it, attempting to further gross them out or increase their fear of touching me, making things much worse for me socially. On the other hand, I was starved for attention and desperate for friends, so even the insult seemed good because it gave me an identity.

Eventually, I would figure out that those traits that drove people away, that led people to scorn me, and that confused and constantly irritated me, were all a part of a hidden neurological disorder. My life has been deeply impacted by SPD, and "Cockroach" is just one of many hurtful names I have been called as a result of my symptoms.

In recent years, I have started to really get to the root of these problems with my occupational therapist. My tactile system has been "rewired" to become much more tolerant of many of the touch sensations I encounter in daily life. OT can make dreams come true. My story has been a testament to that.

And yet, even after my nervous system became more relaxed to these sensations, my mind was still psychologically hardwired into avoiding them. I had to spend time working on removing my beliefs that these forms of tactile stimuli would still be painful. When I accomplished that, however, I was finally able to do the things I once could never bear!

I have finally gotten to a place where brushing my teeth won't send me over the edge. My teeth are in pretty bad shape, and I have had ten cavities; however, I am now beginning to reverse my resistance to dental hygiene. I am also able to appreciate a daily shower. Even if I never truly enjoy these things, being able to do them without them wreaking havoc on me and sending me into a state of overload has been amazing.

SENSORY PROCESSING AND SHAMPOOING

Many everyday activities involve more than just one of our senses. In a shampooing scenario, the tactile, proprioceptive, and vestibular senses play important roles. Visual, auditory, and olfactory sensations get into the act, too. SPD may make these hair-washing steps problematic:

- Feeling the water's temperature and pressure on your head (tactile)
- Turning your body in the shower to see, reach for, and

grasp the shampoo bottle—and not the conditioner (vestibular, visual, proprioceptive, tactile)

- Unscrewing the cap (tactile, proprioceptive)
- Squeezing the bottle for the just-right amount of shampoo (proprioceptive)
- Feeling comfortable with the gooeyness and aroma (tactile, olfactory)
- Screwing the cap back on the slippery bottle and returning the bottle to its shelf while positioning your head to keep water and lather out of your eyes (tactile, proprioceptive, vestibular)
- Lathering your whole head (tactile, proprioceptive)
- Tipping your head back to rinse out lather (vestibular, tactile, proprioceptive)
- Feeling (and even hearing) when your hair is squeaky clean (tactile, auditory)

When Dan was a tween, tactile overresponsivity affected getting dressed, washing up, brushing teeth, and tolerating touch. He was stuck: starved for attention, desperate for friends, self-harming, hopeless, hapless, helpless. Fortunately Dan got the help he needed, and today he is a successful Web developer and an effective "doer" with a wide network of friends.

Sensory overresponsivity can sabotage an adolescent's grooming. So many details to be careful about, to avoid, to endure! So much mental and physical energy to invest!

Developing a bathing-brushing-deodorizing routine takes practice. Where overresponsivity means feeling every sensation intensely, as is usually the case, underresponsivity means not noticing sensations much at all. Here, Avigail writes a refreshing story about how appropriate treatment helped her underresponsive daughter to blossom. (We'll hear more about Daisy in chapter 7.) Strong parental support can be a big help.

FINALLY CONNECTED AND FLOURISHING
AVIGAIL ROBERG, DAISY'S MOTHER

Fashion, hygiene, cool stuff, and hanging around were not part of Daisy's itinerary. She hated hair ribbons, flowers, ruffles, and the femininities that I adore and wanted my girl to like, too. Daisy was the plain Jane with an increasingly intense personality.

When I mentioned this to the pediatrician, who considered me to be complaining, I was told that being nonmaterialistic is a fine attribute and that I should count my blessings. I did, with a hole in my heart—for something was way off, and nobody seemed to understand.

Daisy's voice was subdued, her step was too heavy, her acne was horrid, and she didn't notice or care or, for that matter, feel it, and she picked the pimples until they bled and had acne plus fungus. Refused to put on cream or go to the dermatologist, and because she was so sensitive, I chose not to rock the boat.

Eventually, one of the many professionals to whom I'd written for advice suggested putting Daisy into an OT program. Following my heart and instincts, I jumped in and called an OT immediately. The OT was the first one to truly understand. On the phone, she said that Daisy was probably suffering from SPD. The phone assessment proved correct when they met and Daisy had a full-scale evaluation.

Daisy, at age eighteen and a half, began an intense course of occupational and physical therapy designed to address SPD. It is now eighteen months later, nearly forty thousand dollars incurred for therapy being paid off slowly, and worth every penny. We have included a hatha yoga regimen twice a week. This gentle form of yoga involves physical exercises known as asanas, or postures, designed to align skin, muscles, and bones. This combination of treatments has given her a beautiful figure, light step, sweet voice, sparkle in her eyes, clear skin, super judgment, excellent thinking and analyzing skills, a bright future ahead of her—and the "oddities" are long gone.

Daisy is thriving, loving, connected, and flourishing into a true young lady of grace and note, and I have a new daughter. I can laugh again.

SENSORY SMART SELF-CARE FOR TEENS AND YOUNG ADULTS

Lindsey Biel, MA, OTR/L

Lindsey evaluates and treats children and adolescents with SPD, ASD, and other developmental challenges. She is coauthor of *Raising a Sensory Smart Child: The Definitive Handbook for Helping Your Child with Sensory Processing Issues* and author of *Sensory Processing Challenges: Effective Clinical Work with Kids and Teens*. Go to www .sensorysmarts.com for more of Lindsey's suggestions.

When it comes to self-care tasks, as with everything sensory, you'll need to figure out what are the underlying sensory challenges, determine what can and needs to be changed, and increase your ability to handle a wide variety of experiences. Self-care tasks, such as brushing your teeth, washing your hair, getting a haircut, shaving, and wearing makeup can be profoundly difficult or even painful if you have sensory issues. Fortunately you can change some variables to make the experience "sensory smart."

Let's consider brushing teeth, a problematic self-care task for many people with SPD. Ask yourself:

- *What specific sensory demands of the task give me trouble?* Do an activity analysis of the task, breaking it down into its sensory components. Does the toothbrush hurt your gums? Does the taste or smell of the minty toothpaste with artificial sweeteners gross you out? Does the foam make you gag? There are different kinds of toothbrushes: ones with soft, medium, and hard bristles, as well as vibrating toothbrushes and even finger brushes. There are many types of toothpaste: some do not foam; some taste and smell like chocolate, strawberry, mango, or cinnamon. Lots of choices can make this required task more tolerable.

- *Does the environment play a role?* Is the bathroom light—typically fluorescent—too bright, flickering, or buzzing? Does sound bounce around the tiled room? Is the room too hot or too cold? A fluorescent light fixture can be replaced with an LED or incandescent light with a dimmer switch, or you can turn off the overhead light and use a floor lamp or indirect light from the hallway. You can add fluffy towels, a rug, or even a terry-cloth outer shower curtain to help absorb echoes. You can play music or watch a video while you brush your teeth. You can warm up the bathroom by briefly running a hot shower. Make the environment sensory friendly for you.

- *Do you feel safe and secure?* Rather than standing while dealing with the challenge of toothbrushing, sit more comfortably at a table with a spitting bowl and a cup of water, or wear a weighted vest or compression garment. Finding what works for you takes a bit of trial and error, but once you realize how many variables you *can* change, your sensory experiences *will* change.

More Self-Care Tips:

1. Hate washing and brushing your hair? Start by desen-
   sitizing your head with a deep pressure massage on
   your scalp, ears, neck, and face. An oral vibrator on
   your cheeks, jaws, and lips may help, or try a vibrating
   hairbrush. After shampooing (possibly with an unscented shampoo), use hair conditioner, firmly mas-
   saging your scalp. Conditioner coats the strands to
   make hair easier to manage. Try a wide-toothed detan-
   gling comb rather than a prickly brush.

2. Feel off-kilter when you tilt your head back to rinse
   your hair? Try tilting your head forward, holding a
   washcloth over your eyes with one hand and using the
   other to rinse your hair. This position helps if you hate
   the light touch feeling of water sprinkling on your
   face. If closing your eyes decreases your body awareness, get a tub chair from a medical supply store or
   drugstore. If you are still miserable, try a no-rinse
   shampoo.

3. Dread getting your hair cut? Visit the haircutter first
   thing in the day so there is less likelihood of lingering
   odors from hair dye and other stinky salon products.
   Bring an old shirt to wear over your clothes instead of
   the haircutting smock. Bring earplugs or sound-
   canceling headphones to block out noisy hair dryers
   and blasting music. Also, some haircutters make home
   visits.

4. Hate to shave? Many different types of razors and
   shaving creams are available. Cheap disposable razors
   are more likely to irritate and nick your skin, so your

best bet is to invest in a good razor (electric, if you like vibration) and a shaving cream with a texture and scent you like. Take a hot shower first to soften up the hairs. Desensitize your skin using deep pressure to massage on the shaving cream. If you can't stand touching the shaving cream, use cake shaving soap and a brush.

5. Considering makeup? Less is more. A dash of lip gloss and mascara are often best to gild the lily and they feel less masklike than a layer of foundation, eyeshadow, eyeliner, blusher, and lipstick. You will definitely need to experiment to find the texture and smell of different brands that work for you. Health food stores sell unscented makeup and other beauty products with fewer irritating chemicals. Remember that *no* makeup is absolutely okay. True beauty comes from within!

The stories in this chapter offer a glimpse of what it's like being inside a teenager's skin. If we asked one hundred teens, we would hear one hundred different scenarios, all with the same theme: SPD makes personal hygiene and grooming really hard. What helps? Seeking advice from people who know about these things, growing up, and learning simple strategies to take control can make the job easier.

COPING TIPS FOR COMMON GROOMING CHALLENGES

Everyone is different, so if one of these suggestions works for you, that's great. By trying the others from time to time, you may find your nervous system is changing and you are getting accustomed to sensory stimuli you once could not tolerate. (My thanks to the many adolescents and young adults, parents, and therapists whose strategies are woven into the lists of tips that appear throughout this book.)

IF SPD MEANS YOU DON'T NOTICE OR TEND TO IGNORE UNPLEASANT BODY ODOR OR BAD BREATH:

- Designate a friend to let you know if you need a shower. Promise that you will have no hard feelings.
- Try to find a deodorant or cologne with a nice smell and view it as your "signature." Use it after you shower and before leaving the house.
- Since it may be hard to detect if your clothes are smelly, after each wearing, pop your clothes into the laundry hamper to be washed.
- Brush your teeth after breakfast and before bed. In between, swish with mouthwash or suck on breath mints to minimize bad breath. Floss, too. Then other people won't move away from you because of bad breath, and you will have fewer visits to the dentist.

IF YOUR SKIN AND HAIR ARE BOTHERED BY TOUCH SENSATIONS OF WATER, SOAP, ETC.:

- Position the shower head so water won't hit your face and hair.
- Twist the showerhead to correct the pressure for gentler or more intense water pressure on your skin.
- If you're not shampooing today, put on a shower cap or bundle your hair so it won't get wet and you won't have to deal with drying it.

- Hang a towel over the shower curtain rod. Immediately after wetting your face, you can dry it off early because the towel is at the same level as your head.
- If patting yourself with a towel is irritating, allow enough time to "drip dry" or put on a cotton robe to absorb the water.

IF THE SMELL OF SOAPS AND SHAMPOOS BOTHERS YOU:

- Check that all soaps, shampoos, and body cleansers in the shower stall or bathtub are unscented. If they do have a scent, be sure that their bottles are closed so the aroma rising in the heated space won't irritate you.
- Make certain that your hands are soap free before getting them near your eyes and nose.

IF GETTING WATER ON YOUR SKIN AND SOAP IN YOUR EYES BOTHERS YOU:

- Hang a towel over the shower curtain rod. Immediately after wetting your face, you can dry it off early because the towel is at the same level as your head.
- Rinse all soap stuff off your hands when you rinse your face and eye area.

IF YOU HAVE NO PATIENCE FOR STYLING YOUR HAIR OR KEEPING IT FROM LOOKING WILD:

- Get a haircut every month.
- Choose a simple style that needs no blow-drying, fussing, or hair ornaments.

IF YOUR FINGERNAILS ARE RAGGEDY:

* Keep them clean and short with the appropriate instruments—nail clippers, cuticle nippers, and an emery board file. Look on the Internet for "manicure tools."

* If possible, get manicures (and an occasional pedicure). This is for good hygiene and self-esteem, not just for vanity.

IF YOUR SKIN IS DRY OR VERY SENSITIVE:

* Massage coconut, tea tree, or sesame seed oil into the skin and, if possible, let it soak in for about twenty minutes before bathing, to reduce dryness and irritation. This is a good way to calm your nervous system, especially in dry winter months.

* Use hypoallergenic and unscented soap and skin care products without preservatives.

IF TOILETING IS A PROBLEM:

* Is it an interoceptive issue? You may be underresponsive to sensations of when you need to urinate or defecate. Make a schedule, set your watch, and try to use the toilet every day at the same time to help you become better regulated.

* Is it tactile? Sitting on a padded toilet seat or using flushable wipes instead of toilet paper may feel more comfortable.

* Is it vestibular? If the toilet seat wobbles, secure it by wedging a washcloth between it and the toilet bowl edge. If your feet dangle, rest them on a wooden crate

or a commercial "toilet stool." (You can find this online.)

- Is it proprioceptive? Use a crate or toilet stool. With
  your feet grounded and knees raised, you'll get the job
  done better, as squatting is a more natural and effective position for this activity than sitting upright.
- Is it auditory? Lay a rug on the tile floor to lessen
  acoustically bright sounds. Wear headphones and listen to calming classical music. If flushing sounds like
  you're under Niagara Falls, wash your hands first,
  then flush, and move out fast.

IF MANAGING HYGIENE WHEN YOU MENSTRUATE IS A PROBLEM:

- Carry sanitary pads or tampons and wipes in your
  bag, so you will be prepared if your period starts when
  you are away from home.
- Consider using a menstrual cup, rather than pads or
  tampons. You may need a few tries to get used to in-
  serting it, but it will reduce tactile sensation and you
  may find it very comfortable. Many women with SPD
  call this device a lifesaver; others think it's "skeevy"
  (gross and weird). It all depends.
- If your flow is especially heavy at night, you may need
  to wear a tampon and a pad to avoid messing up your
  bedsheets.
- Learn your flow pattern and plan accordingly. On
  "heavy days" you may need to attend to your hygiene
  every hour. On "light days," you may need to set a
  three-hour check-in.

IN ADDITION:

- When clothes, shoes, backpacks, and other personal items get worn, torn, and dirty, get rid of them. Don't wear rags.
- Stick to a routine in the morning to help you stay on target and not get distracted. After you dress, enjoy breakfast as your reward.
- Create a visual schedule for your morning tasks and stick to it—whether or not you feel you need it! Visual schedules may seem childish, but even adults with organizing issues swear by them. Think of the actions—or inactions—where you tend to get stuck. On file cards, write an action and add a picture. Your schedule cards for grooming may include:
  - Shower
  - Shave or put on makeup
  - Use deodorant
  - Brush hair
  - Use toilet, flush, wash hands
  - Floss and brush teeth

CHAPTER 5

Finding Comfortable Clothes

Ready to greet the day yet? Not quite. After washing, combing, and brushing, after shaving, flossing, and flushing, comes another daily hurdle: getting dressed.

For many people with SPD, clothes are among the biggest irritants. They can feel like the Enemy. Except for the softest fabrics, most clothing materials scratch or burn. Collars rub. Waistbands and shoelaces are too tight or not tight enough. Seams, tags, rough textures, and chemicals in the fabric or wash water may irritate teenagers' skin, literally "rubbing them the wrong way" or "ruffling their feathers."

SHIVERS UP MY SPINE
JASON FISCH

I think that it is essential to be comfortable in your clothes, but I always have trouble finding clothes that are comfortable for me. You would often hear me say, "I don't like the tag's feel against my skin," "It's too tight," and, "When this material brushes against something, it makes a sound that puts shivers up my spine."

Isn't it interesting that the sound of a certain material can cause shivers? The rustling of synthetic fabric may sound as noxious as chalk screeching across a blackboard and may bring on an uncomfortable feeling on the skin and hair follicles. This audio-tactile interaction is called multisensory integration. It occurs when stimuli from various sensory systems simultaneously come into your brain to help you form accurate perceptions of what's happening around you.

Clothes can also smell bad. And certain colors and patterns may be visually offensive. Buttoning, zipping, tying, and getting into and out of clothes may be laborious. Additionally, static cling, the "electrical noise" of clothing, may be highly irritating to the nervous system. Subtle static electricity bothers everyone, especially people with SPD.

Some teens with sensory challenges like their clothing loose; others like it tight. Some like it hot, preferring layers; others like it cold, wearing shorts, T-shirts, and sandals in winter. Some fumble with their clothes or don't realize how the clothes are sitting on them.

What begins as a neurological issue may develop into a psychological one. When kids are little, they can't express their discomfort in words, so they express it in behavior. Frustrated and miserable, they writhe, scream, and pull off their clothes.

Meanwhile, parents "pull out their hair." They may not understand that SPD is the underlying reason and that the child's complaints of pain and discomfort are based on real sensations. Numerous parent-child arguments focus on a child's clothing choices, resistance to new clothes, sloppy dressing, slow dressing, or no dressing. Mary Ann Conway told me that she always struggled with itchy clothes. When she would yank them off, her mother told her that she was going to send her to a nudist colony.

No teenager appreciates hearing "Just get over it," or "Wear what I say is appropriate," or "Who cares how it feels? Don't you care how it looks?" Every teen's position is, "To become an independent adult, I must learn to make my own decisions," while the parent's stance is, "I am responsible for keeping you warm, safe, and presentable." When SPD is present, a squabble over what to wear can escalate into a huge battle.

SOCKS—MY ARCHNEMESIS
EMBER WALKER

I have never been able to tolerate getting my clothes wet. If any part of my clothes gets wet, as silly as I know it looks and sounds, I can feel it and the clothing needs to come off ASAP!

Short-sleeve shirts and shorts take me ages to get used to because I have a hard time tolerating the feel of the air on my arms and legs. I know this makes no sense to everyone else, but, yes, you can feel the air!

Socks were my archnemesis. I refused to wear them unless I absolutely had to. To explain the feeling, it literally felt like razor blades on the tops of my toes. Instead I chose to go barefoot or wear flip-flops until there was snow on the ground! (Oddly enough, if I could force myself to wear socks, my shoes had to be tight so I could feel the pressure. Not normal tight. So tight that I would occasionally bruise the tops of my feet.)

I can remember many a morning that my mother, sweating and crying, would send me to school after physically fighting me to wear socks. The morning fights were traumatizing for both of us.

Until teenagers are mature enough to take charge of what they wear, parents do the best they can, even if they don't know the reason for their kids' idiosyncratic style of dressing—or undressing. Some parents wash the same well-worn clothes every night, buy acceptable clothing items in duplicate or triplicate, or sew clothes in the patterns and fabrics that their kids can tolerate.

How else do experienced parents cope with SPD clothing issues? They learn to accept that sensory difficulties cause the behavior; it isn't the child's fault. They avoid conflicts about clothes, saving their energy for more important topics, such as taking on responsibilities or not engaging in risky behavior. And they let comfort reign, as a comfortable kid is more likely to be relaxed and engaged.

COMFORTABLE (IF NOT COOL)
DEBRA EM WILSON, SHALEA'S MOTHER

For teens with sensory issues, the typical experiences that most teens find enjoyable are a mixed pleasure or downright miserable. Five years of OT-SI helped Shalea immensely, but some areas remain difficult, and learning to thrive in high school when you are a teen with sensory issues is a day-by-day experience.

Before high school, she attended a small school in Shasta, California. When I learned that the high school housed 1,500 rambunctious, hormone-inspired students, I didn't know how we were going to get through her first week, let alone four years!

The first challenge was getting her dressed to look like a typical teen. Most teenagers want to wear the coolest clothes adorned with name brand chic. Tight jeans and even tighter T-shirts.

Going shopping for the first day of school is an exciting day for most teens. Not for mine. During a quick trip to the mall, I patiently cajoled her into trying on new clothes. When that didn't work, I just about forced her into the dressing room. Begrudgingly, she acquiesced.

Leaving the store, bags in hand, I rejoiced that I had pulled it off. I was thrilled at the possibility that she was going to look like the other teens. I breathed optimistically, hoping she and her nicely fitting clothes would make a good impression.

The first day of school was upon us. I eagerly anticipated seeing Shalea in one of her new outfits. But my high hopes fell to a deflationary low, as she came to the breakfast table in her old, worn, comfy sweats. She said simply, "Mom, I like my sweats. They're comfortable. The other clothes are too tight."

So back to the store I went, exchanging the "cool" clothes for sweats and hoodies in different colors so she could wear a variety of outfits each week. To go with the casual sweat and T-shirt look, she fashions her hair in a ponytail daily because the hair bothers the back of her neck when it is down.

On picture day, she had her hair in a ponytail and was wearing her sweats. That's her look, and that's fine for now. I have three more years to convince her otherwise for her senior portraits! Wish me luck.

How do other teens with SPD learn to cope with clothing issues? Some get treatment to desensitize their skin. Most learn, as they mature, to express themselves verbally about why certain clothes are unwearable. They develop strategies, such as slow breathing, going outside, or getting heavy, deep touch pressure into their bodies to get through the discomfort. They discover that it's up to them to become the "boss of their own body."

A splendid example of a young adult coping successfully with clothes is Kori Cotteleer. Here's the background to her story.

As a girl, Kori wanted nothing but air to touch her skin and hair. Now in her early twenties, she no longer struggles with clothes, thanks to OT-SI and strong support from her family and therapists.

Kori has held a special place in my heart since she was six. I learned about her hard times when I met her parents, Marla and

Joe, in Chicago. I was there to speak for Sensory World about how SPD plays out in young children's home and school life.

Marla and Joe had just heard about SPD. No doctor, teacher, or professional had suggested SPD, but a close family friend with knowledge about sensory issues mentioned SPD as a possible cause of Kori's behavior and handed them a conference brochure. In the brochure, Marla and Joe read a list of SPD characteristics, many of which described Kori.

They came to the conference. During a break, they strode toward me and, teary eyed, introduced themselves. They told me about Kori's difficulties. Marla said, "My poor child has to do so much juggling and planning to get through just one hour of her day . . . Last Christmas, she said the only present she wanted was for her sensory problems to go away."

At home, Kori resisted being touched by clothes, sheets, hairbrush, and people. (Interestingly, caring for the household menagerie of bunnies, cats, dogs, fish, and lizards that she grew up with was a pleasure, because she was in control of the touching.) She had tactile issues at school, too. When Marla helped in the classroom, she noticed that Kori couldn't sit on the floor next to other children, had to be first or last in line, and refused to use the bathroom because she said the soap felt "icky" and the paper towels were the wrong kind.

Marla noted, "But the teachers didn't think those were real problems."

The school wasn't helping, except for a smattering of OT to improve Kori's immature fine motor skills, e.g., poor cutting and illegible printing. Sporadic school-based therapy, however, would not address what went unrecognized: severe tactile dysfunction. Kori made little progress.

As we talked, Marla and Joe pressed into my hands a three-minute video of Kori furiously resisting putting on new clothes.

They hoped I would use the video as a learning tool to show future audiences what life was like in their home every morning, because nobody seemed to understand. (I started showing the video to spellbound and often weeping audiences all around the world. With arresting clarity, the video shows the sort of tactile over-responsivity that Kori and her family struggled with every day.) Even sympathetic pediatricians, relatives, and friends were as mystified as Marla and Joe.

A few weeks later and after speed-reading every book and visiting every SPD website, Marla got Kori started with occupational therapy with a sensory integration approach (OT-SI). Marla also implemented a sensory lifestyle program at home, with lots of deep touch pressure and proprioceptive input.

It worked!

Marla wrote: "We have just begun the program, and my little girl has made remarkable progress in every functioning aspect of her life. The anticipatory anxiety, which has been the secondary component of her tactile problem, has almost entirely diminished. Already, she is wearing new underwear, new shirts and pants . . . and also allowing me to put her hair in pigtails!"

This was thrilling progress to hear about. Kori was making great strides and growing more in sync each day.

Over the years, I lost touch with the family. A decade passed, and I was back in Chicago to speak, this time for the STAR Institute, then called the SPD Foundation. Lucy Jane Miller, the organization's founder and research director, suggested trying to locate Kori; maybe she still lived in the area and would like to attend the conference.

Miraculously, we found the family, and they came—not just to listen but also to speak. Now it was Kori who strode toward me, arms extended. "Carol, thank you for helping my family. May I give you a hug?" she said. "Because I'm a hugger now."

This time, I was the one with teary eyes.

Kori's story is profoundly meaningful to me. Below, she tells us what it was like growing up with SPD.

YOU *HAVE* TO WEAR JEANS
KORI COTTELEER

In high school, I could spot kids who seemed overwhelmed by sensory stimulation. They looked like I used to look before I got treatment. I would introduce myself and tell them I thought I knew how they felt, and we would talk, and I could give them some suggestions. I became an SPD advocate. I was voted Most Friendly and Most Involved by my peers. Nobody ever won two awards before. I'm telling you this because when I was three, a therapist who knew a little but not a lot about SPD told my mother that I might never be able to read or write due to my severe sensory disorder.

I used to hate wearing clothes. Clothes felt like millions of needles were poking me. I never wore socks, never wore gym shoes (only sandals, all year, even in winter). I wore only certain outfits, if anything at all. (At home, I stripped.) I went through many phases in life as far as my—let's just call it, "condition"—goes. I wanted to wear jeans, but I couldn't. I had to quit dance class and gymnastics because I couldn't wear a leotard or tights, and the recital costumes were way too scratchy. I didn't last in soccer; between the shin guards, socks, and shoes—well, you can imagine.

I also hated certain things touching my body: wool or thick blankets, scratchy rugs, lotion, and worst of all, underwear. I did not wear underwear. At a parent-teacher conference, my teacher told my parents that I could have a career in the nightclub business!

It hurt not only physically, but also mentally to wear clothes and shoes. I wanted to scream and moan, and I scratched my skin until I bled. I would scratch so hard because the pain of cuts felt better than what the clothes felt like on my skin. I wanted to wear what my sister and everyone else was wearing, but I couldn't because it just was so unbearable. It was torture. My parents used to hold me down to dress me until I was too tired to fight and was worn down enough to leave the clothes on.

Going shopping, I had to feel inside the clothes. That was how I judged whether I'd be able to try them on, let alone actually wear them. After I bought and wore clothes a few times and they started getting pills, which are like little collections of fabric and fuzz, I had to stop wearing them because they were painfully scratchy. Even my sheets and pillowcases felt so bad on my skin that I tried sleeping standing up or on the wood floor. On family road trips I used to sit in the car with just a thin cotton blanket on, and we had a van, and my parents would keep the window shade down, the whole trip.

What I did like: "worn-in" pajamas, my dad's big T-shirts, water, sand, rice, shaving cream, swinging, standing on my head, being rolled over and under the big therapy ball. Loved OT. Loved deep pressure. Once I had clothes on, I liked to be hugged hard for a long time, to use the therapy ball, and to feel someone's weight pushing against me.

I was overresponsive to most tactile sensations and at the same time underresponsive to temperatures. I could walk barefoot in the snow and take burning hot baths til my skin would turn red.

After seven years of intense OT, I overcame my sensory disorder, because of several very special and dedicated individuals: my OTs, parents, brother and sister. My condition was a family ordeal, so everyone helped. They took turns rolling over me with a big exercise ball the second I put my clothes on, or they would push me against a wall or hit me with pillows til my clothes felt okay. They would help me get dressed and able to leave the house every day. At night everyone would push on me to give me deep pressure. We had lots of pillow fights. We had indoor and outdoor trampolines and an indoor bar swing that I loved hanging upside down from and swinging on. Not only would I hang upside down, I also slept upside down. It just felt right.

My mom would go to conferences to find out what she and my teachers could do. She spent a lot of time educating my teachers about my sensory needs, and most were cooperative. The teachers and school nurse would give me very hard, tight hugs every hour. I would carry my class library books from my classroom to the library because carrying heavy things helped me feel better. My gym teacher let me wear my very cute Pocahontas sandals instead of unbearable gym shoes, and even the recess ladies stopped worrying about my feet getting cold in my sandals.

Fortunately, I have fought through my clothing aversion, and now I can wear whatever I want without feeling like I am being tortured. What really helped me was people's willingness to learn. My teachers, my friends, my family all took hours trying to understand how I was feeling and what they could do to help.

My final, intensive OT session was for a solid week, five to six hours daily. I brought bags of clothes in to help desensitize me so I could wear them. As I got older my desire to wear what everyone else wore played a huge role, too.

Another big motivator was my desire to ride horses. You *have* to wear jeans to ride. That's when I put my first pair of jeans on! I was determined, so I put them on for one minute, which was all I could stand. The next day, I put them on for two minutes. Finally, I could tolerate them for a couple of hours. Then I went to the stable and soon became a pretty good rider.

That desire to ride helped me persevere along with the motivation and support of my family and friends. They told me I could do it, and I did!

The adage "Bad happens so good can come of it" comes to mind as I review stories like Kori's. The "good" that came of very bad tactile overresponsivity includes her appreciation of family and therapists, her advocacy for peers with SPD, and her determination not to let SPD rule her life. More mature and able to control important parts of her environment, Kori is in charge now.

COPING TIPS FOR COMMON CLOTHING CHALLENGES

IF SPD MEANS THAT MOST CLOTHES MAKE YOU UNCOMFORTABLE:

- Buy clothes a size too large; they will give you less skin friction. Girls, if you like looseness, wear your dad's big cotton shirts when relaxing at home.
- Or, if snug clothes are more comfortable, wear bodysuit shapewear underneath.
- Wear your favorite soft shirt or leggings underneath your outfit for increased comfort.
- Be sure underwear is neither too tight nor too loose. Look for underwear with cotton covering the elastic. A gentle elastic effect around the waist can be helpful, but you don't want the waistband to bunch on the skin or to impede natural belly breathing. As many people have subtle allergies to latex, check that none is in the elastic.
- Search online for seamless clothing. When seams are unavoidable, wear socks and underwear (including bras, if possible) inside out.
- Look for tagless shirts (probably invented by someone with SPD!) to avoid the irritation and stinging that may drive you nuts. In clothes that still have tags, carefully remove them with a seam ripper to get all the little pieces—do not rip them out.
- Avoid collars and cuffs with constricting buttons or

elastic. Wrists and ankles are very sensitive, and so is the neck. (As Peter Sullivan, whom we'll hear from in chapter 8, says: "Who invented the tie anyway? It's just one step away from a noose.")

- Don't buy something if you have doubts about it. You're not going to wear it, no matter how great it looks on you, if it makes you feel uncomfortable. Don't think you must wear anything that will drive you up a wall.

- If you find a clothing item you love, buy several right away before they run out of your size or discontinue the style. Then you will always have something to wear that just feels good.

IF SHOES ARE PROBLEMATIC:

- At home, go barefoot, or wear just socks. Out and about, wear shoes with flat soles or very low heels, as high heels may cause postural alignment problems in the back and neck.

- Choose the right shoe size (maybe a half size large) so that your feet are unrestricted and have a full range of motion. Also pay attention to thermal comfort and venting for shoes.

- Try wearing leather shoes with no socks. Not only does the leather feel good, but the conductive animal skin also helps manage static and "electric noise."

- If you have flat arches in your feet, add arch support to avoid throwing your legs and especially knees further out of alignment. Shoes with built-in arch support or adding an insole with support may help.

- Avoid trendy footwear that offers no support, such as slip-on foam clogs and pull-on sheepskin boots. These can worsen preexisting flat feet and pronated ankles and may lead to clumsiness, poor posture, a poor gait, and even a torn meniscus over time.

IF YOU FUMBLE WITH CLOTHES:

- It may help to get dressed in front of a mirror.
- No mirror? Start buttoning a shirt at the bottom, which you can see.
- To improve sensory-motor skills, practice handling three-dimensional objects without looking at them. (Andrew Short, who has discovered that playing blindfold games can improve activities of daily living [ADL], offers more ideas like this at http://blindsen soryexploration.com)
- Try exploring in your wardrobe or buttoning up a shirt while blindfolded.
- Sort dry pasta and beans.
- Mingle buttons with beans in a "sensory bin." Close your eyes, or put on a blindfold, and feel around for the buttons. To make this more challenging, Andrew suggests putting small buttons or coins into "a messy texture that will get all over your hands, like very soft Theraputty, or cream or baked beans or cooked pasta." After this activity, buttoning a shirt will be a snap!
- Use clothing as a tool. Wear heavy boots or clogs (or ankle weights from a sporting goods store) to ground you and help you become more aware of where you are in space. Weighted jackets and heavy jewelry may help you feel calm and get more accurate sensory information about where your body parts are.

- Use hooks or nonslip hangers. Hanging up clothes that you do not choose to wear is an important habit to develop, especially if you try on lots of clothing to find something comfortable to help you make it through the day.
- Put away clean clothes in stacking bins, labeled "Underwear," "Shorts," etc., instead of tossing them all into a messy drawer (or on the floor).

IF CLOTHES IRRITATE YOUR SKIN OR MAKE YOU FEEL IRRITABLE ALL OVER:

- Wear clothing made from 100 percent natural materials, such as cotton, bamboo, and leather. (Wool is natural but usually too itchy, especially right next to the skin.)
- Avoid 100 percent polyester clothing and poly-cotton blends. Most have a static electric field that sensitive people can feel. Wearing these sorts of clothes may make your nervous system feel "creepy."
- Wash clothing several times before you wear it the first time. Some of the chemicals that are used in the manufacture of fabrics can cause rashes and often smell bad to sensitive people. Use only natural or hypoallergenic and fragrance-free detergents. Put ½ cup baking soda in the wash cycle, or ½ cup white vinegar in the rinse cycle, to soften fabrics and remove static cling. (Commercial clothing softeners are typically toxic and will irritate the skin and noses of many people with SPD.)
- Consider buying "preconditioned" clothing from a consignment or thrift shop.

- In the house during the winter, use a humidifier to keep humidity in the range of 40–60 percent to reduce static and prevent dry, itchy skin.

- Pay attention to your body temperature and the room temperature to maximize comfort and find the range for peak performance. When you are going back and forth between indoors and outdoors, wear layers of clothing to put on or take off.

- Find activities involving deep pressure that desensitize your skin and feel good, such as having someone push against you, being rolled over and under a big therapy ball, and relaxing under a weighted blanket.

CHAPTER 6

Eating In, Eating Out

Eating is so crucial for life that it engages every sensory system simultaneously. Eating is usually physically and emotionally satisfying—and even fun.

For those with SPD, however, eating can be the opposite of fun. It can seem like a chore or a punishment or an enemy that cannot be ignored. Often, a teenager with SPD comes to the table reluctantly and picks at the food, eating just enough to get by and hoping nobody will notice.

A PICKY EATER—TO SAY THE LEAST

JASON FISCH

One of my worst SPD traits was my eating and food texture challenges. Eating was one of my biggest obstacles I had to overcome. As a child I was a picky eater, to say the least. I had three major food groups. First of all was chicken fingers with ketchup. Second were French fries. Last was drinkable yogurt. As you can imagine, this wasn't the healthiest diet. The texture of most other foods was what bothered me the most. As I have grown up, I have learned to cope with texture by thinking about only the flavor and washing down tiny bites of unappealing food with big sips of water.

If I go to a friend's house to eat and there is something that I particularly don't like, I always politely decline. Also, I tend to have a little snack before going so that I am not famished and feel like I have to eat.

I FED IT TO THE DOG
DEBRA EM WILSON

I was a sensory kid myself, but in the olden days, nobody really knew anything about it. I suffered many a car trip totally sick to my stomach from an overresponsive vestibular system. I have always been a picky eater.

My parents made me sit at the table for hours forcing me to eat food that I couldn't get down due to my tactile issues. I didn't go near certain textures of food, no matter the consequence.

Back in the day, many parents followed the "tough love" philosophy of child rearing. My dad insisted that I eat what was put in front of me. My mom, understanding more than my father, would whisper, "Feed it to the dog."

When Dad left the table, I'd do an under-the-table hand-off to our poor dachshund, who would have benefited from a weekly Overeaters Anonymous meeting. He became quite plump eating my sensory distasteful leftovers!

Going out to eat may be extremely hard on teenagers' sensory systems. When eating is the focus, they may choose to decline dates, preferring to stay home where the food and environment are predictable and safe.

NO THANKS TO THE TACO PLACE
JUDY MCCARTER

I have always had stomach issues. Spicy, greasy, fatty, and tart foods have never agreed with me. Healthful foods are better, but when I was a teenager or in college, nobody went to health food stores or out to eat at nice organic restaurants. I would eat the stuff my dates so proudly provided me, and then I would go home and get sick. Several times I declined dates because those fellows liked to go to the taco place.

Sitting at family meals, going to restaurants, and attending parties where food is served are experiences that one twelve-year-old boy says is "like being in jail."

In the SPD world, picky eaters abound, eschewing a wide variety of food for a wide variety of sensory reasons. (See the following box.) Stir in any undetected food intolerances—and the result is a very selective eater.

SENSORY PROCESSING DISORDER'S EFFECT ON EATING

Because eating engages all senses simultaneously, SPD can make this essential activity uncomfortable or even intolerable. Here are some sensory reasons that eating may be difficult.

- **Visual:** Seeing certain foods may evoke previous bad eating experiences. Or foods on the plate may touch one another, which is Not OK, or their color may be objectionable, or they may "just look gross."

- **Olfactory:** Smelling greasy or aromatic food may make the overresponsive person gag or feel nauseated.
- **Gustatory:** Food that tastes too sweet, bitter, spicy, etc., may be nauseating.
- **Tactile:** The feel, texture, and temperature of food matter greatly. Some overresponsive people won't eat soft and smooth food. Others won't eat lumpy, crispy, chewy, seedy, or grainy food, or hot food, or cold food. The teen with underresponsivity or poor discrimination may be uncertain about what is in his mouth and whether he has chewed sufficiently to swallow it without choking.
- **Auditory:** Hearing others take bites, chew, slurp, and swallow may be painful. This condition is known as misophonia, literally, "hatred of sound." Many people with overresponsivity to sounds prefer to eat alone.
- **Proprioceptive:** Positioning the hands to use utensils to cut and the jaws to chew food may be difficult for the person with poor proprioception and decreased muscle strength.
- **Vestibular:** Sitting upright at the table may challenge a person with inefficient vestibular processing and low postural tone. Or the person may crave movement and be unable to sit quietly for long.
- **Interoceptive:** Digesting food or even the anticipation of eating may be distressing. An overresponsive teenager may dread the feeling of a full stomach, for example, or avoid foods that may cause an upset stomach, constipation, or diarrhea.

Tactile overresponsivity is the most common reason for eating issues. Many teenagers with SPD dislike anything with a mushy or a crunchy texture in their mouths. Others are very particular about flavor.

ONLY BOLOGNA
KERRY MAGRO

For a long time I had food I would not eat, like tomato sauce, and would eat only bologna sandwiches. I would not eat anything mushy like mashed potatoes and pudding.

Patience was one of the biggest things for me when it came to eating certain foods. My parents, who used reward systems, would often encourage me to try a food a few times, and if I didn't like it I'd never have to eat it again. When it came to all the food groups, though, with luck I always liked at least one item.

I DO NOT "DO" FLAVOR
EMBER WALKER

When I was growing up, eating was never pleasant. I abhorred anything remotely spicy, disliked candy passionately, and usually avoided crispy things. Drinking was the same—nothing too sweet, nor too cold, and even pop was too fizzy for me.

I do not "do" flavor in foods. I tend to like things bland and avoid even candy because it is too flavorful. Anything that set off those parts of your mouth when you're eating sweet or sour candy or a savory steak was my enemy. That feeling you get in your mouth can make me nuts.

For ages I resisted chewing gum or eating taffy, tomatoes, squash, and watermelon because of the texture. And, yes, before you ask, watermelon has a terrible texture!

What can parents do when the texture, taste, smell, sound, or sight of food disgusts a kid? They want their kids to eat, especially if they are aware of how important good nutrition and a healthy sensory lifestyle are for developing a strong, well-regulated nervous system to support efficient cognition and behavior.

Good nutrition includes a variety of fruits and vegetables, meats and fish, eggs and cheese, beans and nuts, grains and seeds. When foods like these are missing from a selective eater's diet, so are sufficient amounts of essential minerals that a growing teenager needs for brain development, muscle contraction, energy production, and so forth.

Kelly Dorfman, a clinical nutritionist, suggests supplements to provide minerals such as zinc and magnesium. (See box on page 98.) Zinc is needed to support the immune system and reproductive health. Magnesium protects the nervous system from becoming overloaded. Magnesium supplements can protect teenagers from hearing damage and auditory processing difficulties that are often caused by deafening music blasting through their earbuds.

But parents learn fast that forcing food or lecturing a child about eating mineral-rich mushrooms and asparagus won't work. Nobody can make another person eat—or sleep, or poop.

What seems to work best is listening and talking to tweens and teens when they are old enough to be treated like partners with a common problem to solve. (To hone your problem-solving skills, refer to Dr. Lucy Jane Miller's approach, A SECRET, in chapter 12.)

Also, take heart that when kids reach the age of eleven or twelve, eating habits often improve for several reasons. Physiologically, taste buds change with maturity. Foods that tasted terrible a few years ago may taste good now. Socially and emotionally, adolescents are readier to expand their list of acceptable foods, one tiny bite at a time, because they long to belong. They want to go to pizza parties like everyone else. Cognitively, as they begin to accept ownership of their SPD, they change their attitude. They often become motivated to make peace with more foods so that their picky eating habits don't stand in the way of friendships and fun times.

GETTING OLDER HELPED
JUSTIN WAYLAND

I am sensitive to foods—taste and texture. I don't like it when a food mixes textures—for example, crunchy nuts in soft brownies. I also don't like it when things taste different than I expect. Recently we bought a new brand of milk because our old brand wasn't available. I did not like the new brand, because it didn't taste the same.

I've learned that new foods are overwhelming at first, but you sort of get used to them after a while. That usually takes a long time. I wish my parents had known that if I don't like a new food the first time, I probably won't like it the next day, or even for the next few months.

When I am confronted with a new food I try not to "judge a book by its cover." Sometimes new foods taste good even though they don't look very good. For me, taking a zinc supplement made things taste better. Also, getting older helped.

THE OUT-OF-ZINC TEENAGER

Kelly Dorfman, MS, LND

Kelly is a licensed nutritionist/dietician. In her clinic, she uses nutrition therapeutically to improve brain function, energy, and mood. She has helped many children and adolescents with a cornucopia of eating issues. See www.kellydorfman.com for more information on nutrition.

Most kids with SPD have higher sensory and nutritional needs than typical kids. They have not only a poor sensory lifestyle but also poor, self-limited food diets because of overresponsivity to textures, smells, and tastes.

While a good sensory lifestyle program—an individualized activity plan designed by an OT—is critically important to correct sensory processing imbalances, its effectiveness is limited by the quality of the connections making up the neural network. If the nervous system is composed of "malnourished" wires, sensory therapies may be insufficient to produce efficient sensory integration.

Picky eaters' preferred foods are often either crunchy or creamy. The Crunchy Diet consists predominantly of white or brown processed foods like pretzels, peanuts, popcorn, French fries, crackers, and chips. The equally popular Creamy Diet is heavy on milk products, bread, plain pizza, and pasta. Foods like dark leafy greens, beans, seafood, mushrooms, and avocados, which are rich in zinc and magnesium, are not welcome on their plates.

Many picky eaters complain that food "smells bad" or "tastes funny." These are the rationales they use for rejecting your famous chicken dish or a different brand of yogurt. Some kids will not even sit at the table with the rest of the family because of the offensive dinner smells.

One popular view of this phenomenon is that people with SPD are super-tasters, equivalent in talent to the sommelier at an expensive French restaurant. Not true. All of the picky-eating "super-tasters" I have taste-tested need visual or contextual cues to accurately identify a taste. They need to see the slight change in color of their preferred yogurt or feel the texture of the peas in the casserole to trigger their aversion.

That is not to say that food does not actually smell or taste "off" to them. The problem is their taste and smell experience is out of sync. We do not know exactly what they are tasting or smelling, but a ripe banana may taste not sweet but sour to them, for example. Or onions being sautéed smell like vomit rather than the beginnings of a delicious dinner.

These super-sensitive tasters/smellers are usually picky eaters with a mild *zinc deficiency*. With a zinc supplement, the excessive number of foods with "off" smells and yucky flavors may be reduced to a normal level. (Like everyone, kids still prefer some smells and flavors and avoid others, so not liking onions is not necessarily a sign of zinc deficiency.)

To test for zinc, a doctor can request a specific blood test. A simpler idea is for parents to go online and buy a zinc-testing solution to screen for deficiency. The zinc sulfate solution tastes like disgusting, old eggs to people who do not have a deficiency—and it tastes just fine to people who do.

—Adapted with permission from the book *Cure Your Child with Food* (2011) and articles published by Developmental Delay Resources

While some teens don't eat at restaurants or parties, others do but in a way that embarrasses them and strikes their friends as rather odd. They may give lengthy instructions to a waiter about how they want their sandwich, or studiously push anything green to the edge of their plate. They may binge on chips to get proprioceptive input and get full so quickly that they throw up. Bingeing and vomiting may then raise questions about whether the adolescent has an eating disorder—a "look-alike" condition for which SPD is frequently mistaken.

SPD may make some foods disgusting or threatening, but having heightened senses is not all bad when it comes to preparing food. Some young people with SPD become interested in nutritious food and creative cooking because of their sensory differences. To get food that's palatable, they must make it. They often find that cooking is a pleasure and that they are good at it. Also, the kitchen may be an oasis where they can busy themselves productively, be in charge, and find a little space away from the noise and commotion of an overstimulating gathering. Their cooking skills turn out to be a bonus for everyone in the family.

AMAZING KNACK FOR COOKING
EMBER WALKER

Unlikely as it seems—despite avoiding flavors, spices, and textures for most of my life—I have an amazing knack for cooking and recipes just based on smell or, if I'm feeling gutsy, on a quick sample of whatever I'm making. I learned that as long as I knew the texture or the taste of something that was coming, it wasn't quite so bad. I became the family cook and now run a blog where I even share some of my recipes. Everything I went through was for a reason, and all my struggles were worth it.

Everyone should feel comfortable and welcome at mealtime. An important goal of many families is helping adolescents feel comfortable and unpressured so they can "come to the table"—not only at family meals, but at school, at parties, and at other social gatherings. Usually, adolescents and young adults with SPD have the same goal, and once they can make their own decisions about what and where to eat, whom to sit down with, and in some cases what to prepare, mealtimes begin to feel a lot less like punishment and can bring a lot more joy.

COPING TIPS FOR COMMON EATING CHALLENGES

TO COPE WITH EATING ISSUES AT HOME, HAVE A FAMILY POWWOW ABOUT WAYS TO MAKE MEALTIME MORE PLEASANT, LIKE THESE SUGGESTIONS THAT HAVE HELPED SOME YOUNG PEOPLE WITH SPD:

- Involve all participants in preparing food that they like, or setting the table.
- Dim the lights or eat by candlelight.
- Always put some food on the table that the choosy eater finds acceptable.
- Designate a Pasta Night, when everybody at the table begins with a similar plate of plain spaghetti. Set out bowls of sauce, sautéed vegetables, grated cheese, etc., for people to choose exactly what they want.
- Listen to quiet, soothing music (from speakers rather than headphones) to block out some environmental sounds and stay socially engaged.
- For every family member who can't sit for long, get a therapy ball, a ball chair, or an inflatable seat cushion to sit on instead of a standard dining room chair.

- Don't talk about food during a meal but instead discuss current events, upcoming vacation plans, or an experience during the day that made the speaker feel glad, sad, or mad.
- Play games such as Two Truths and a Lie, where everyone gets to tell the family two things that really did happen at school or work and one thing that did not.

IF SPD CAUSES YOU TO BE UNCOMFORTABLE EATING OUT, BUT YOU WANT TO BE MORE SOCIABLE:

- When invited out for dinner, ask what will be served and how many others will be there. Knowing what to expect can make a huge difference in how you experience and respond to the gathering.
- Eat at home before going to a social gathering. Then, at the party, you can honestly say you just aren't hungry.
- If the dishes that will be served are Not OK, eat a snack before going. When you are there, take small portions so your plate is not empty, and eat what you can. Being present shows that your friends' company is the nourishment you value most.
- When you find a restaurant that serves food you like, but the place is too noisy or crowded, go with a friend, and order food to go. Eat on a quiet park bench or take it home.

TO BECOME MORE PHYSICALLY COMFORTABLE WITH EATING:

- Before eating, get some deep pressure, such as pressing your hands together or down firmly on a table. Press your feet into the floor, hard. Wrap your arms around yourself and give yourself a great bear hug. Squeeze your shoulders, arms, hands, legs.

- Throughout the day, try getting oral input, such as sucking applesauce or a thick milk shake through a straw or chewing, carrots, bagels, or granola bars. Rub a Nuk brush inside your mouth and use a vibrating toothbrush to lessen tactile overresponsivity. Vigorous oral input may soothe and calm some people.

- Amuse yourself during long family dinners by playing a chewing game that Annette Himmelreich invented, which featured her grandmother's chewy, dried-out brisket: Chew on the right side of your mouth once and then on the left side once, then the right side twice and the left side twice, and so on. Thinking about the game may distract you from the taste and texture.

- Pick one new food to work on. Don't get overwhelmed by presenting yourself with a menu of new foods that you feel you must learn to tolerate. Take it one food at a time, one day at a time.

- Take a small bite of a new food today, and tomorrow, and the next day. If you cannot bear to bite and chew it, first try rubbing it on your lips, and then try licking it. Some foods take a while to get used to, but the effort is worthwhile to broaden your list of acceptable foods.

CHAPTER 7

Heading Out into the World

Say it's Tuesday, an ordinary day. Say you are an adolescent with SPD. Say you have coped pretty well this morning with getting up, showering, dressing, and eating breakfast. Those tasks demanded a great deal of planning, strength, and stamina, but you got them done. Now it's time for the next uphill task—heading out the door.

To people without sensory issues, leaving the house is not a problem. We put on our coat, go out the door, and walk, drive, or take a bus to our destination. For many with SPD, however, stepping out of the house is a much bigger operation.

Here are some reasons that a teen may find going out to be challenging:

- Physically, transporting oneself from point A to point B is difficult. Driving, taking the bus, or just walking down the street may be unnerving due to sensory distractions and irritations.
- Cognitively, planning and sequencing multistep transitions may be hard. Changing from warmth to wintry air, from quiet to cacophony, from Mom to a mob, can be especially taxing for teenagers with dyspraxia and impaired self-regulation.

- Emotionally, home feels reliably comfortable and safe, but out there, discomfort awaits. The world may seem unpredictable and confusing, not enticing. Anticipation of real or imagined pain or obstacles heightens anxiety.

This story in the form of a letter explains what it takes for one young person with SPD to get out of the house each morning.

STEW OF SIGHTS AND SOUNDS
RACHEL S. SCHNEIDER

Dear Reader,

I am not unlike you. We ease out the front door, the wind blowing softly, and our neighbors are still tucked in bed. If you do not have SPD, it is here we part ways.

Perhaps you glide forward into your day with some sense of stability and poise. You run for the bus, make room for another straphanger, jump off the bus, mingle with the throng at the post office, breathe in the scent of cinnamon as you near the bakery.

I, too, plunge into the world outdoors. The crowd of people in the street looks like sharp, intersecting lines—painfully bright and colorful. The girl next to me at the crosswalk whispers into her phone as a fire truck blares past us. The sounds intertwine, seem to ricochet off the storefronts, and make me wince in unidentifiable pain. It is a stew of sounds and sights, and suddenly my heart is beating faster and my palms are sweaty. The world around me shifts in size—from very wide to very tight, and back again.

I am terrified. I walk fast to get through the sights and sounds that make me jolt, practically stomping, as I reach the subway stairs. I somehow stumble over the first step, nearly landing face-first on the ground.

My shin is bruised. By the time I get where I am going, I feel completely drained of energy and simultaneously jumpy.

Your day may begin like mine—if you have sensory processing disorder. If not, welcome to the morning of someone with SPD.

The barrage of auditory and visual stimuli overwhelms Rachel. Not surprisingly, it stirs up an intense fight-flight-fright response.

Not only do sounds and sights assault her and other overresponsive people, but also smells may be particularly irritating. Our sense of smell is our oldest and most primitive sensory system, which our ancient ancestors used first to warn them of danger. We are capable of discriminating one trillion sensory stimuli (Bushdid, et al. 2014); most of us use our olfactory sense less than we could. Some overresponsive people, however, with their extrasensory abilities may smell things whether they want to or not. They tell me that cigarette smoke, body odor, perfume, and smells emanating from garbage cans, tailpipes, and restaurants' exhaust systems can bother them even when they are a good block away.

In her book *Sensational Kids*, Lucy Jane Miller says that an ordinarily benign scent "can trigger sweating, an increase in heart rate, shallow breathing, and other physiological reactions that are normally seen in the presence of a real danger, such as a snarling dog." With that kind of overresponsivity, leaving the house is anything but simple.

Striving not to scream, striving to hold it all together and to get in sync . . . why, just walking down the street can be exhausting. Feeling at the mercy of one's environment and not in control of one's own body is frightening. Self-regulation can be hard work.

ALTERNATIVES TO SCREAMING
CHLOE ROTHSCHILD

Let's pretend that I am walking on a crowded street, and it is very loud with a lot of people. Since I don't like either of these things and struggle to self-regulate, I yell at the people to "shut up and get away from me!" This is not considered to be an appropriate response and is likely to make people around me think bad thoughts about me, as well as to have other unwanted consequences.

As I've grown, I've learned better responses [included among those at the end of the chapter] that are a lot more socially appropriate than, say, yelling at people, which one may do because of not knowing a better way to self-regulate. If your body feels funny and uncomfortable, you are going to do anything you can to make it feel better. If screaming makes you feel better again, and you do not have any other strategies readily available in your brain, then you will probably use the one that is most familiar to you, screaming.

Leaving the house can be unsettling, yet it must be done. The world awaits. With support, determination, and preparation, it is possible to get out there, taking one small step at a time.

GOING OUT IS LIKE CAMPING OUT

Paul Balius

Paul Balius has grown up with SPD. He has been a machinist, engineer, and building architect and presently works as the director of information technology for a large manufacturing firm. For fourteen years he volunteered in a prison ministry in three California prisons and continues counseling and preaching in a home church. He also mentors young men, helping them to reach their potential in life.

Sensory challenges can make going out of the house the equivalent of roughing it on a camping trip. You want the new experience but dread the discomfort you will endure.

You may develop strong fears of anticipated pain, akin to the dread of backpacking in the wilderness in difficult weather. The worrying about possible ways to suffer may become as bad as, or worse than, the actual suffering. You may be trading the joy of participating in life for the security of not having to worry.

As we grow up, it's easy to accumulate bad experiences, each one marking something else, like a crowded bus, as off-limits. You don't want to risk enduring that pain twice. But learning to become isolated and hide out at home is the wrong lesson. The right lesson is learning how to avoid the select things that are hurtful so we can get out into the world.

Imagined discomfort is one reason that going out is hard. Another reason is that home is known, whereas outside is always unknown. Take one step outside, and who knows what will happen? You cannot control a world out of sensory control. At home, you have far more control in the privacy of your room. Yet staying locked inside is merely imprisonment, where the only crime was being born with a strange sensory system. It hardly seems like a fair punishment for nothing done wrong. We need to pardon ourselves and step into the freedom we deserve.

I love the quote "A journey of a thousand miles begins with a single step," by the Chinese philosopher Lao-tzu.

For the sensory constrained, each day's journey begins with taking one more step beyond our sensory prison. Preparation is critical. In the same way we wear a coat to protect ourselves from getting cold and wet, we need to find fresh ways to care for those unique senses that are exposed and need protection, too. Don't ever give up, because you will find new ways and will never regret trying.

To explore new experiences and live life more fully, we all have to be a little uncomfortable. And though you may be camping out on rough terrain for a time, the starlit sky makes up for every pebble you lie upon.

If walking down the street can be nerve-racking, what about driving?

Typically, adolescents champ at the bit to get their driver's license—freedom, at last! Driving allows them to get to places without having to hassle with annoying people and sensory challenges. Teenagers with SPD and perceptual-motor difficulties may feel they can control their environment better when they are in the driver's seat—literally and figuratively. Driving confers control, comfort, convenience, and cachet. Driving turns the corner from childish dependence to adult autonomy.

What's not to like?

Plenty, for some teenagers with SPD! They may proceed with caution even when they become eligible to drive. They may worry that their sensory issues could take a huge toll on their sense of well-being. In addition, their inefficient perceptual-motor skills could be a roadblock to competent driving. (See the following box.)

PERCEPTUAL-MOTOR SKILLS INVOLVED IN MOTORING

Drivers must process innumerable sensations rapidly and accurately. When senses are out of sync, perceptual-motor skills may be inefficient, too. Driving a car—or "motoring"—involves these perceptual-motor skills (defined in chapter 2, "Primer"):

- Regaining equilibrium after going around a curve (balance)
- Steering with both hands on the wheel (bilateral coordination)
- Using eye-hand-foot coordination to start the car and shift gears (laterality)
- Using the correct foot for braking and accelerating (body awareness, laterality)
- Being aware of where you are in town and where you are headed, without depending on the GPS; parallel parking (directionality)
- Starting the ignition; locking/unlocking the doors; adjusting the windshield wipers; using dashboard buttons (fine motor control)
- Braking; twisting to see behind you (gross motor control, midline crossing)
- Putting on your seat belt; turning the steering wheel around a long curve (midline crossing)
- Getting in and out of the car; shifting gears; changing lanes; getting to your destination (gross motor control, praxis—sometimes called "motor planning")
- Backing out of the driveway; staying centered in your

> lane; threading your way through a turnpike toll-
> booth; weaving through traffic; gauging your distance
> from other cars; obeying traffic signals (visual-spatial
> awareness)
> • Interpreting street sounds, horns, sirens, and screech-
> ing brakes; understanding signage (auditory-language
> skills)

On top of their physical challenges with sensory processing and perceptual-motor skills, teenagers may be concerned about environmental distractions. One big distraction is driving with passengers,
especially peers, whose presence increases a teenager's tendency to
drive fast or recklessly (Chein, Steinberg, et al. 2011). More distractions that pile up and are out of their control include rain and snow,
slick roads, potholes, other vehicles, and pedestrians.

Many overresponsive adolescents ("sensory avoiders") are risk
avoiders. If they don't want to drive but need to go places, a solution
may be to have a parent drive, to take public transportation, or to
practice, practice, practice until driving becomes easy. Where there
is a will, there is a way to get out of the house, even if the way is a
little inconvenient. Here, some of our writers discuss their driving
decisions.

DRIVING WAS TOO SCARY
NICOLE WOLSKE

In high school, other girls were excited about getting to drive. Driving
was too scary for me, so I held off getting my license until after college.
My teen and young adult years were tough because I didn't learn to

drive until I was twenty-eight. I always had a fear that I would crash or get into an accident. I was pushed to get my license, and when I finally did, it was great for a while, but I haven't driven much, because I still have that fear... what if...

YOU DON'T HAVE TO PUSH YOURSELF
EMBER WALKER

I learned to drive on an old brick road, away from people, cars, noises, etc. My mom taught me there. She always kind of knew I didn't do well with too much of anything. So I think this was her way not only to make sure that I was learning safely, but also to help me foster self-confidence in driving and feeling comfortable enough to drive, period.

Mom tried to teach me how to drive her stick shift once. I just could not motor plan, plus pay attention to the things you need to when driving. I pulled halfway into the driveway after that lesson, left the doors wide open, and ran inside, completely overwhelmed. So I *had* to drive an automatic car—that much was clear. This was my solution to problem number one—my poor motor coordination.

Problem number two was my surroundings. I learned to avoid busy streets, because there was just too much going on for me to be able to process the movements, the noises, the lights, and so on. Since I can't control my environment, nor remove myself from an overstimulating issue, I learned to just take different routes and keep off streets that are always busy or packed at rush hour.

Problem number three was weather. Sunlight flashing through trees is seriously maddening and still sends me to anger very fast. I've solved this visual problem by avoiding driving unless the sun is coming up, going down, or straight overhead. I don't drive in snow, ever, and rarely in the rain. You have limitations when the seat belt is like sandpaper, your sock seams are like razor blades, too many brake lights are going on and off, and noises from outside or within the car are extremely distracting. My solution? Get someone else to drive when it rains or snows.

To deal with unavoidable problems while driving, I learned to sometimes just pull over and breathe. You can deal with things, without losing it. You can push through the discomfort a little bit and find something that works. It's okay to just stop and regroup. You don't have to push yourself past the breaking point.

There is a spectrum of driving ability just as there is a spectrum of sensory processing. For some, driving is a challenging and even overwhelming ordeal. However, others with SPD love to drive and, after much practice, learn to do it well.

EASY ROADS

Temple Grandin, PhD

Temple Grandin is well-known as a person with autism as well as an author, advocate, and innovator. Her many books include *Temple Talks . . . about Autism and Sensory Issues* (2015) and *The Autistic Brain* (2013).

Because of my sensory challenges, I have difficulty with multitasking. To get around this problem while learning to drive as a teenager, I spent a year on easy roads until operation of the car became automatic, and I no longer had to think about how to steer or step on the brake. This solves the multitasking issue. After a year on easy roads, I gradually went into more and more traffic and out on the freeway. I suggest new drivers try this method.

Another road to successful driving, aside from lots of practice, is getting appropriate treatment. When SPD affects motor coordination, posture, and balance, for example, learning to drive can be a formidable challenge. Therapy may help many drivers like Daisy.

BALANCING THE DRIVER
AVIGAIL ROBERG, DAISY'S MOTHER

At her graduation, I noticed with alarm that Daisy's posture was off. All the other girls in the marches were standing straight and tall, and she was not. Pediatrician ruled out scoliosis.

Hard time, and I felt that when the real structured school environment ended, it was as though the curtain fell down in the middle of the play. It was time to revise the script, retrain the actress, or enter a new stage.

Driving lessons were dragging on, and she couldn't get it—many hours, many dollars, and zero achievement. Frustration, disappointment, anxiety, and negative energy filled our home, although I was trying to be positive.

We opted for a therapist specializing in anxiety who found her charming, not suffering from what he termed "anxiety." Rather, he noted her inability to maintain a balance of independence, codependence, and dependence that are so vital to friendships, and this imbalance could be very challenging for her. Dead end—or so I thought after spending $350 for a two-hour session!

It took a few days, and then the lightbulb went off in my head. If Daisy can't maintain balance in an abstract form, why should we think she can do this in a physical fashion?

Then Daisy began a program of OT and hatha yoga, which is a comprehensive and integrative form of occupational therapy and physical therapy, creating great balance and very affordable. Marvelous improvements occurred.

Our journey has yielded the observations that weak core strength and poor postural alignment create significant challenges in sensory integration, motor planning, and motor function. The anxiety therapist had been bang on. Although he couldn't explain the connection, Daisy could not balance! Driving was initiated after four months of OT... and now Daisy is an excellent driver!

SPD AT SCHOOL, AT WORK, OR AT THE MALL

On foot, in a car, or on a bus, the adolescent or young adult with SPD eventually arrives at his destination—at school, at a job, at the mall. Uninvited, SPD comes along for the ride.

Teenagers may not know they have SPD, but they do know that something foils their efforts to get places, learn in class, and complete their work. On any day, it is hard enough just to exist, and then it gets much harder because it is necessary to *coexist*! In busy settings, comfortable coexistence is an elusive goal.

A common complaint is that most people "just don't get it." While parents, teachers, classmates, and others probably notice the adolescent's unusual behavior, e.g., screaming when a door closes or fidgeting constantly, they frequently don't recognize the underlying problem.

After all, people with SPD don't look different. They may be beautiful and handsome, intelligent and creative, thoughtful and humorous. They may be capable of doing well the particular things that interest them greatly. They may be capable of doing adequately the many things that must be done. At school, for instance, they can get to class, grasp complex information, express their thoughts verbally, read and write, assemble their three-ring binders, and do homework and pass it in on time. But for some reason, they are often clumsy and disorganized.

Here is what may be happening.

Some individuals with SPD need more time to accomplish a task because their sensory processing is slower than their peers'. Some need a quieter, dimmer room because sounds and sights overwhelm them. Some need more space because proximity to other people makes them uncomfortable. Maybe they can't finish a task in one sitting because they need frequent trips to the bathroom. Maybe in a social situation, words come slowly, or words fail them. Maybe they isolate themselves because they hate being noticed for their quirky behavior and then scolded, laughed at, or bullied.

Until sensory issues are addressed, being in school, work environments, and public places can be hell. But then, when sensory issues are addressed, things often begin to change for the better.

The stories in this chapter touch on recurring obstacles: unawareness of SPD at home and school; feelings of being judged and harassed; and problems dealing with noise and other sensory issues. But the picture is not totally gloomy. We'll also look at factors that can turn things around for the better: parents' awareness and attention; appropriate therapy; and a growing determination among young people with SPD to improve their lives and develop their talents.

THE MESSAGE: I DID NOT MEASURE UP
DEBBIE FEELY

My handwriting and map coloring were illegible because of poor fine motor skills. My classmates with pretty hair and nice, smooth skin knew how to color maps beautifully within the lines, and I wondered why I was not like them. Teacher after teacher commented how oddly I wrote. Even in college, the freshman English professor suggested I just pack and go home.

Poor gross motor skills hampered my moving like the other kids. I wondered how they knew what to do. Throughout my school years the constant message from teachers was that I did not measure up. The school had tryouts for a new choir, and I was one of two in my class not chosen; I had no idea why. My world did not make sense.

Other than a few notes on report cards about me crying at school, nobody ever recognized a problem. Quite the opposite: I remember a high school teacher who was delighted to provoke me, poking me with his pointer. I hated him calling attention to me. He said I had to get over being shy if I wanted to survive.

I hated it, but I am grateful for it. In response I went out and got involved in student leadership.

Unfortunately, Debbie did not have the support she needed because she grew up in an era when parents and teachers were unaware of SPD. Children and teenagers who do get support at school and especially at home fare much better.

FINALLY I CAN CONCENTRATE
IAN HOYMAN

My SPD applies to the ear, so noises such as pencils and papers rustling are magnified, and I have trouble concentrating. I used to go to a school of around three hundred students. But I could not handle it. Ergo, I became overwhelmed and in considerable pain, remarkably so, during breaks and recess. When I told my parents, they said that I needed to learn "social skills." This is hard. I have no idea whether people hear and experience like I do.

Whistling hurts me because of the frequency and pitch, and it sometimes puts me into a rage, although I don't know why. The kids would whistle on purpose to hurt me. They thought that I was lying or that it was interesting to see me react. It took all the restraint I had not to flat-out attack. I had a few other personal problems, too.

My parents found a better school for me, and finally in eighth grade (what I am currently in), I can feel at home. The classes are small, and finally I can concentrate.

There are many people who believe sensory processing disorder is a lie or a delusion or even a phase. SPD exists!

People need to know. I would still be in pain if I did not express how painful having SPD actually is.

To anyone who embodies sensory processing disorder, I urge you to disclose this to any person in your life whom it applies to and who needs to know, whether it be a teacher, parent, employer, or even fellow worker—or else nothing—or anything—at all will happen.

To handle my SPD, I listen to soothing music and play around with relaxing items, e.g., Chinese therapy balls that ring. I play the double bass, and it is a soothing instrument to me. It is beautiful and plays deep.

Young people with SPD have a leg up when their parents are determined to understand their kids' problems and help find solutions. They have an even greater advantage when their own resourcefulness grows and they discover what they can do for themselves.

For instance, Ian's parents enrolled him in a smaller school more attuned to his needs. His father, a bassoonist, introduced his son to the double bass, and Ian finds it is soothing therapy to play the bass and also to handle ringing Chinese balls.

Justin (next) is a teenager whose drowsiness at school puzzled everyone. Although his teachers couldn't understand why he became sleepy and slow moving, his parents figured out that noise affects him intensely, sometimes causing him to experience complete sensory shutdown. (Shutdown is nature's way of protecting an overloaded nervous system.) Justin discovered that he could solve the problem by wearing earplugs in the noisy corridors and making a beeline to get to class on time.

BEELINE
JUSTIN WAYLAND

My biggest sensory challenge is auditory. My hearing is sort of okay 90 percent of the time, but the other 10 percent of the time I become hideously aware that something is wrong. For example, I become aware that I can't understand what the person next to me is saying because there is so much noise. Or I will be listening to something loud, like an orchestra or band, and I will start to feel very sleepy.

Walking in the hallway between classes at school is really hard because it is so noisy. It makes me feel sleepy, and then it is hard to get to class on time. A loud hallway is a problem for everyone, not just for someone with auditory sensitivity.

When I go away from the noise, I start to feel awake again. Minimizing my exposure time helps—I finally learned to beeline to my next class so I could get away from the noise quickly. Earplugs are helpful, too, because they block out the noise and make it more bearable.

For Andrew Herbert, another young man with sensitive hearing, paying attention and learning at school was a struggle. When he told his parents what it was like to be overresponsive to auditory sensations, they were all ears. They got him started with listening therapy and other treatment to normalize the regulation of his central nervous system. As we'll see, the outcome has been a great success.

AN ACUTE EAR
SALLY HERBERT, ANDREW'S MOTHER

Andrew had not been formally diagnosed with any particular label. He attended an Episcopal school with a hands-on academic setting that was tailor-made for him. Yet, at every parent-teacher conference, we would hear: "If only he would focus and pay attention, my gosh, what he might be able to accomplish!" He was thought of as an underachiever because of his inconsistent learning patterns. He came across like an absentminded professor and kind of "ditzy."

But because he was very bright, he was chosen for a program allowing sixth graders to take the SAT. He scored high enough to get into college—as a twelve-year-old! Yet he could make 100 percent on a test, and the next day, on the same kind of information but in a different setting, make 30 percent.

"You are not trying hard enough," and, "You are not putting forth enough effort," he heard. He was a frustrated learner and was frustrating to teach. All the teachers knew in their hearts that Andrew "could do great things." They just were not sure how to draw the best out of him.

When the teachers collected baseline information, they found that Andrew did not consistently stay on task and pay attention. He visibly clicked on and off, two to three hundred times, in each class. Baseline for staying on task was close to 0 percent in sixth grade.

Then we learned about Dr. Guy Berard's work in France with children who had hypersensitive hearing. At twelve and thirteen, Andrew had auditory integration training (AIT) and began to tell us about some of the differences that he saw in himself.

Andrew thought that what we hear and process was the same for every person. He knew he had a hard time coping with all the noise but thought that everybody else heard the same noise and could somehow handle it better.

Andrew shared some other enlightening thoughts with us. He

said, "Why do you think that I did so well on the SAT? Because it is the
one day that the teachers demand quiet—you can't shuffle your feet,
you can't move your hands, you can't move your desk, and if you do,
someone will come and make you be quiet. All the directions are short,
and with that kind of information, you can click on and off. Perfect for
me.

"Why do you think I study best with fast-paced music? To get my
engine running and to focus.

"It was worth getting a detention at school for not finishing my
work, so I could take my homework home. The other kids shuffling papers, the principal talking on the phone a few doors down, people
walking, and trucks gearing down outside—it's all too distracting.

"Mom and Dad, you don't know it, but I get up in the middle of the
night when the house is quiet to do my homework. I can work when
there are no dogs barking, no pots and pans clanking, and no phone
ringing.

"I hear people walking down the street and understand their conversations. I hear my eyelashes blink and my heart and lungs pump. My
world is way too loud to live in."

Wow! For parents that hadn't a clue, this was a lot of information to
take in!

Once the therapy took effect and his hypersensitive hearing set-
tled down, he was left with acute hearing for music, and that is why he
was such an excellent music student and performer. His processing
difference ended up being a benefit!

Now he has completed his master's in music. His major professor
noted that Andrew was the most gifted student that he had encoun-
tered in his thirty years of teaching. When we, as parents, heard that
comment from an unbiased person who knew nothing of Andrew's
background, we were bursting with pride.

Andrew currently loves teaching music composition at the community college, working with those very professors who saw the great

potential that he had to connect with people through music. He is proud of who he has become and does not want any child to go through what he had to endure. We were glad that we found the exact help that Andrew required, allowing him to grow and flourish into an exceedingly talented human being.

The "absentminded professor" grew up. Andrew's auditory difference became an asset, and he became a skilled educator, in tune with his students. Like Shonda, the graceful dancer, and Ember, the creative cook, Andrew used his extrasensory talent as a vehicle to success and a better life. The next story is from another adult reflecting on how a special interest in sound and music helped him to succeed at school, fit in socially, and guide children with visual and other sensory difficulties like his.

USING MUSIC TO LEARN AND INTERACT
CHRISTOPHER SABINE

I am significantly visually impaired and grew up with severe sensory processing difficulties in a place and time when SPD was unknown. I was very sensory avoidant, proprioceptively, vestibularly and especially tactilely. I physically resisted my parents' and teachers' valiant attempts to teach me fine motor skills such as buttoning and tying my shoes.

Growing up, I was unable to tolerate and learn Braille initially, which really set me back in school. My first attempt to learn it was a nightmare. Touching the dots felt like rubbing my fingers on abrasive sandpaper. I had more than a few meltdowns in class when vision teachers tried to make me focus on reading or writing it.

With years of daily living skills training and OT, I did learn to read

Braille and also to dress and tie my shoes. Finally, in my twenties, I could process the texture and design of the Braille alphabet, and I began to read books.

During my final, successful attempt to master Braille, memories of my initial attempts as a child came flooding back. Indeed, I would not be able to read Braille had I not had those early lessons—but why were they so hard?

The reason is that they lacked a relation to music and sound—as vital to me as eating, breathing, and social interaction. When I listen to my favorite artists, everything is at peace. The music wraps me in a blanket that is immensely calming but also stimulating. There are no disabilities, cares, special needs, or limitations. I interact with the music and become part of it.

As a child, I associated every life experience—from words and numbers to the sounds of family members' voices—to particular musical tones. These formed the bedrock of my perception of the world. Identifying an object by its tone was vital to understanding its essence and its place in my world.

I became fixated on different sounds that I could discriminate and control. I developed a keen interest in telephones. Near my suburban home, there was some rural phone-switching equipment that interacted to route local and long-distance calls, and I could tell where a person was calling from just by the ring sounds.

I had a special interest in the sounds of car horns and motors. From the time I started speaking, at three, until about six, my favorite word was "beep." Most of my interests revolved around things that beeped.

But at school, my time became increasingly filled with things that did not beep. These included OT, speech therapy, orientation and mobility instruction, Braille, print books, devices to teach me fine motor skills, and, eventually, a closed-circuit television that I began using to read books. Using this TV was very tiring and sometimes led to headaches, but I needed it after attempts to teach me Braille failed because I was so tactilely defensive (overresponsive).

If I could have made people understand my need to connect those different combinations of rough dots with something that beeped, learning Braille might not have been so difficult. It would have been much more interesting if I could have associated the tactile code with the musical tones and sounds in my environment.

But look at me now! As I grew older, I learned that I had to manage my musical interests in order to fit in socially. From fifth through ninth grade, I sang in the school choir and took part in state competitions. I graduated from college with honors, earned a master's degree in social work, and launched a business specializing in services to families of children with my condition.

Some parents are heartsick that their children will never experience the joys of living life visually. They might say, "My child will never see my face." I say that the music and sound around us can be as spectacularly beautiful as any great sunset, painting, or landscape.

When a child whose family I am working with achieves a major milestone, I always listen to some favorite music and reflect on my life's greatest moments and memories of being a child with unique learning needs. I celebrate because I know my insights and experiences have helped a child learn to overcome the challenges I have faced and to thrive.

Auditory and visual processing difficulties are common in people with SPD. Indeed, auditory and visual issues are quite common in all populations, and yet these problems are frequently overlooked. Often, schoolchildren "pass" the vision and hearing screenings because they can see the big E on the chart and hear the little beep through the earphones. But, while seeing sights and hearing sounds (visual and auditory acuity, i.e., sharpness) may be adequate, processing and understanding visual and auditory information may be slow or late or otherwise out of sync.

If detecting visual and auditory difficulties is hard, spotting processing problems with less-familiar senses is even harder. Without knowledge about SPD, what parent or teacher could guess that interoceptive overresponsivity causes a young person to use the toilet frequently? That vestibular craving causes another to rock constantly in his seat? That proprioceptive underresponsivity and dyspraxia cause another student to drop the chemistry beaker?

The story below describes teenage life when Marlene's proprioceptive needs at home and school were misunderstood until she learned about SPD.

PRECIOUS PROPRIOCEPTION
MARLENE GOMEZ

Does it get better?

It did for me.

It certainly does, especially if you have good personal resources, a rich and healthy environment, caring teachers, and loving—and very patient—parents. With these supports, I survived. I call it survival, as that is how it felt and how, in hindsight, I can better express the constant alertness I needed to stay alive.

I did survive first, thanks to my very relaxed environment, where a very "peculiar" child like me didn't face any acceptance problems. Occupational therapy with a sensory processing focus did not exist in Baja California Sur. However, my hometown, La Paz, honored its name: "The Peace." It was a peaceful and accepting environment.

My teachers were always kind to me, even if I had just crawled through the classroom to reach my best friend to talk incessantly. I was never punished nor did my grades suffer just because I was incapable of sitting during the afternoon to complete homework or to take per-fectly tidy notes or focus on things I didn't fancy or already knew.

My mother never minded if I only wanted to wear swimsuits after school. She let me choose all my meals and never bought itchy cloth-ing. My father never really made me feel like a bad child for breaking things or hitting others. They would let me stay in the pool even at 9:00 p.m.

My parents' friends even encouraged me in all my adventures. Climbing into an air force hangar inner structure was one more of my quirky habits, as was biting bullies.

I never felt judged. My self-esteem during those years never suf-fered.

I had had glimpses of the "real world" whenever I traveled to see my extended family in Mexico City, but never long enough to over-come my hometown's fantastic environment and culture.

Unfortunately, my peaceful life crashed like a house of cards when my father was moved for work to Mexico City. I was twelve, and I felt my life had ended. In the new environment, noises at night would keep me up; the cold weather would make me cry and curl into a ball; and cold rain would make me cringe.

I not only had to deal with the hardships of a school transfer, learn-ing a new language (the school was bilingual), and adapting to a new home. Now I look back and see that I lost the precious proprioception I need to stay focused, relaxed, and in sync. Due to pollution, recess was only twenty minutes, with no exercise, and I was expected to re-main seated for five hours and a half!

It was a disaster, which at sixteen resulted in depression, weight gain, loneliness, bad self-esteem, and eternal conflict with peers, fam-ily, and teachers. I coped—I survived—thanks to my cognitive skills, the only thing left. I immersed myself in books, study, and the few friends who shared those interests. I did try to be social, as my early life had given me a taste for social activities, but it was taxing.

Finally, I entered my chosen college and started to breathe again. It was heaven. It encouraged self-regulation, with long distances to walk between classes, a lovely library, and little nooks to be alone for a while. I could choose my schedule, my teachers, how many subjects to take. I had more free time.

I started learning about behavior, cognition, and other strategies. After graduation, I was hired by the Mexican Clinic of Autism. I used my "special" sensitivities to understand and communicate with the children, who, like me, had a hard time touching things, eating a wide variety of foods, and dealing with noises and stimuli in general. Was life as bad as it had been in high school? No, not anymore, I could cope more.

Marlene got therapy and made significant changes in her life. She has become—what else?—an occupational therapist.

The stories in this chapter illustrate how SPD can weigh down an out-of-sync adolescent outside the home, especially at school. Emotional issues, the stresses of puberty, and unsupportive educators increase the load and make it hard not only to coexist but also to learn in a regular classroom.

Most schools are designed for typical students who learn easily using their eyes and ears. But learning is optimal when information enters via all sensory pathways. What if adolescents are predominantly visual learners who choose to sit and read? Or auditory learners who prefer lectures, discussions, and audiotapes? Or proprioceptive learners who must keep moving to absorb information? Or tactile learners who need to handle everything to understand it? Should parents and teachers try to get their teenagers unstuck, or let them stick to their ways?

Jane M. Healy, PhD, author of *Your Child's Growing Mind* (2004) and *Different Learners* (2010), says, "Purposely, and gently, move them just a little out of their sensory comfort zone to ultimately strengthen their skills. It is silly to try and focus input to a learner's 'preferred' style to the exclusion of others. The brain remains plastic throughout a lifetime, and nothing is wrong with asking/helping students to utilize and thus strengthen their less-preferred channels."

Lucy Jane Miller, author of *Sensational Kids* and Founder of STAR Institute for Sensory Processing Disorder, adds, "But do not force them to change. People with SPD cannot just change. They must slowly adapt to that which is noxious to them."

Combining encouragement and practice, practice, practice is best, so that visual, auditory, tactile, and proprioceptive learners, in time, can use all their senses to learn.

When their schooldays are past and workdays begin, young adults' sensory issues do not change. At the office, just as in the schoolhouse, their daily task is to cope with hubbub, confinement, misunderstanding, and underappreciation. Finding work that involves physical activity may be far more satisfying than sitting in a classroom for those who need regular movement throughout the day.

PHYSICAL WORK WORKS FOR ME
ZACHARY PROSSICK-BROWN

A major thing about SPD is that you're not fully aware of where you are in space. I find that putting strain on my muscles makes my brain more aware of my body and helps them work together better, and it clears my mind. I ride my bike every day. I run and lift free weights. I have become interested in my own health.

My best jobs have been physical. When I was in my early twenties, I did landscaping during the summers. I would wake up in the morning, and my fingers would get locked into place as if I were holding a shovel or a rake. I enjoyed that job. It made me strong. It gave me perseverance that I have carried with me. Doing physical work makes me feel like I accomplish something. It suits me.

Currently I am the building attendant leader for a team of custodians. Interacting with and leading my employees has been very challenging at times. I have learned a lot about talking to people and establishing work relationships. Being a janitor is a good job for me. I cannot sit at a computer and cannot stand to be out of shape.

Kids at the college I work at sometimes look down on me. This is because they do not know me. I get the sense that sometimes cleaning workers are looked down upon. Physical work in this country is seen as menial. As if anyone can do it. Some people have to do it. This is a negative stereotype. A garbageman told me once, "If it wasn't for the garbagemen and janitors in this country, celebrities would be sitting in a pile of trash."

I started my job five years ago with a roomful of other people who were getting trained. I'm proud to be one of only four who have remained at the job, and all of us have moved up to management positions.

My life and work experiences have educated me better than school ever did. Don't let school get in the way of your education.

Zack's philosophical approach to his job works well for him. With his high movement quota, he needs daily, vigorous physical activity to keep in shape and in sync. Note that he seeks input but is not a classic sensory craver. He gets organized and feels satisfied with certain sensory input, whereas a sensory craver has an insatiable need for more input.

There is going to school, and there is going to work, and then there is going shopping. Shopping at the mall is an American pastime, and adolescents with SPD want to go, too. But according to numerous contributors, the mall is hardly SPD friendly. This story comes from Jennifer McIlwee Myers, who wrote *Growing Up with Sensory Issues: Insider Tips from a Woman with Autism* and is an advocate for people with ASD and SPD.

MISERY AT THE MALL
JENNIFER MCILWEE MYERS

As a teenager I'd read an article about how "the shopping mall is the new town square and general store," and going to the mall serves vital social and economic functions in the modern American community.

Now, I was rule-bound and tended to look for, learn, and follow rules for doing things. I didn't know I had sensory issues.

So, if I needed a birthday card, socks, or any little thing I could buy at the mall, I saved that errand for Saturday morning. I avoided doing errands elsewhere so that I would have something to do on my mandatory mall trip.

But going to the mall Saturday morning left me so frazzled and haggard that dealing with the little glitches of life was more than I could do. I would get upset and angry even when I really didn't want to be. I'd be unable to let things go, unable to defuse my own anger, and unable to have many weekends where I wasn't an emotional wreck.

After I was diagnosed and began to learn about ASD and SPD, reading about how sensory issues can affect people blew me away. I hadn't realized that those other shoppers weren't experiencing anything like what I experienced. They couldn't hear the conflicting music coming from multiple stores at once; they couldn't smell the full variety of smells that permeated the whole place. They didn't have the constant tension of seeing so many other people moving near them in startling ways, all those little movements of all those people adding up to a chaotic visual overload that made me want to run and yell and scream and go fetal, all at the same time.

Parents who have read my books or heard me speak often ask me, "When we go to the mall, after a half hour my son just lies on the floor and screams. Why does he do that?" The answer I want to give is, "Why don't *you* do that? It's the most logical response to the mall; why is he the only one in your family that understands that?"

Once I understood a bit about SPD, I realized that it was not a good thing for me to go to the mall and that I should excuse myself from going there. Developing this understanding not only made my life (and everyone else's) easier on the weekends, but also made sense of much of my childhood. It made it possible for me to forgive myself for not having "done better" and not having been able to focus on what I was supposed to be learning. It was a major step to making peace with my past.

As Jennifer's story illustrates, an important aspect of developing coping skills is gaining an understanding of what will work for each individual. While our hyperconnected and often judgmental world can seem to dictate how things should and should not be done (especially for adolescents and teens), the truth is that one size often does not fit all. It's essential to figure out what works for each of us so that we can coexist in a demanding world.

COPING WITH COMMON "HEADING OUT" CHALLENGES

IF SPD AFFECTS HOW YOU FEEL ABOUT LEAVING HOME:

- Prepare yourself for the day with an activity that you know will make you feel alert and organized, such as jogging, taking a shower, or chewing a bagel.

- Plan ahead as much as possible. Make a list of everything you will need and check it off—lunch, books, keys, wallet, backpack, etc. Become a strategist to survive in the world.
- When the going gets tough, sit down or pull over—and breathe. Don't push yourself past your breaking point.
- Accept that there will be situations, such as poor weather conditions, that put you on sensory overload and make it very difficult for you to drive or get about. At these times, rely on someone else to get you where you're going, if possible.
- Use the time you spend traveling from place to place to learn new things. Listen to soothing music if you must concentrate on driving. Listen to audiobooks and interesting interviews if you are traveling on the bus, train, or airplane.

IF OVERRESPONSIVITY TO VARIOUS SENSATIONS MEANS GETTING TO PLACES IS HARD:

- Plan outings for times when flickering sunlight, bright lights, busy traffic, or bad weather conditions will not bother your visual system. Wear a visor, hat, sunglasses, or a loosely hooded sweatshirt to block out bright lights.
- Block out loud sounds with earplugs. Stock up on the brand that is most comfortable, and always keep a spare pair handy. Alternatively, use noise-canceling headphones or earmuffs, or listen to instrumental music through an MP3 player or iPod—but only when you do not need to pay strict attention to what is going

on around you or what is being said. Play music softly
to protect your eardrums and allow you to stay conscious of your surroundings. Use the devices in mod-
eration, because there's a world of conversation and
sounds of nature out there to be enjoyed!

- Wear a mask, such as the type designed for bicycling
  in a polluted area, to block out offensive smells.

- Eat a snack so you have a little something in your
  stomach when you leave home to make traveling more
  comfortable.

- Long rides as a passenger can be a hardship. If you
  have motion sickness, Annette Himmelreich suggests
  distracting yourself by playing little games, such as visually "jumping" over telephone wires, trees, or drive-
  ways. Focusing on stable structures will help you cope
  better than gazing out the window at a confusing blur.

IF MOTOR PLANNING AND MOTOR COORDINATION DIFFICULTIES AFFECT YOUR ABILITY TO DRIVE:

- Learn to drive on roads that are off the beaten track
  and preferably out in the open. On easy roads you can
  master how to drive without most distractions.

- If possible, drive a car with an automatic shift, not a
  stick shift.

- Pay attention to how your hands hold the steering
  wheel—firmly without clenching.

- Monitor your sitting position to be sure it is the most
  supportive, with your hips close to a right angle to
  your back. Use a lumbar support, if needed.

- At red lights, stretch your neck and arms.

GENERAL SUGGESTIONS FOR BEING AT SCHOOL, WORK, THE MALL, AND OTHER PUBLIC PLACES:

- Protect your eyes, ears, and nose, as suggested earlier.
- Drape a "lap buddy" (pillow or tube sock, filled with beans or fish-tank gravel) on your thighs or shoulders to provide calming weight.
- When you feel stressed, sit back to feel the support of the chair, let your hands hang loosely by your sides, and inhale to the count of three and exhale to the count of six. Repeat several times.
- To keep awake, to get organized, or to stay calm:
  - Fidget with handheld items that are appropriate for the place, i.e., ringing Chinese therapy balls at home, and quiet pencil-top fidgets and other squeezable, twistable gadgets at school, on the bus, at work.
  - Sit on a T-stool, a Hokki stool, a therapy ball, a ball chair, or a cushion or other seat designed to help people with sensory needs remain alert.
- To provide oral-motor input, suck on throat lozenges or chew gum—the bigger the wad, the better.
- Take thirty-second movement breaks every fifteen minutes. Stretch your arms overhead, widely, and behind you. Twist your wrists in circles. Raise and lower your shoulders several times. Stretch your legs straight out. Flex and bend your ankles and knees. Press your feet into the floor. Press your hands onto the desk. Grasp your wrists and pull your hands apart. Press your palms together. In the classroom and doing homework later, stretch, jog in place, or do a few push-ups against a wall.

AT SCHOOL, DECIDE WHICH TEACHERS TO TELL
ABOUT YOUR SPD SO THEY CAN UNDERSTAND
YOUR CLASSROOM BEHAVIOR. YOU MAY WANT
ALL YOUR TEACHERS TO KNOW, OR, AT FIRST,
JUST ONE OR TWO. THESE ARE SUGGESTIONS OF
THINGS YOU MAY WANT THEM TO KNOW:

* Sensations such as flickering lights, fluttering window
  shades, rustling papers, and scribbling pencils make
  you physically uncomfortable and unable to concentrate.
* The reason you chew gum, fidget, and move around is
  to stay present and focused, not to indicate boredom!
  (Sympathetic teachers may allow you to chew gum
  just for taking tests and writing essays, even if the
  school disapproves.)
* You do best when you know what's coming so you can
  be prepared. A "heads-up" before being called on and
  a syllabus for the term will help you know what information the teacher expects you to master, test formats
  and dates, and when papers and projects are due.
* You need extra time and a quiet room for exams.

TO BUILD OR BROADEN SENSORY PATHS TO
LEARNING:

* Spend lots of time outdoors, ideally in the country or
  woods. Looking, listening, and moving outside will
  enrich your understanding not only of math, biology,
  and earth science, but also of every subject you are
  learning. Walking while memorizing a poem or re-
  viewing French conjugations, for example, reinforces
  what you have read or heard.

- To lock in new information, sniff a lavender sachet or suck on a tart lemon ball while studying for a test. On test day, sniff the sachet or suck the candy, and the olfactory/gustatory input may evoke what you learned while studying. (If you have overresponsivity, this idea may not appeal, but give it a try. If you have sensory discrimination disorder, this idea will help. If you are a sensory craver, you may love it!)
- If you are an auditory learner, push yourself to read about a subject although you prefer to hear about it. If you are a visual learner, listen to an audiotape rather than read about a subject. Use all your sensory options to learn.

SUGGESTIONS FOR WORK:

- Listen to instrumental music, without lyrics, when your work involves reading and writing and you need to concentrate. Classical music or jazz, for example, may be just right. Wear earphones if necessary.
- Listen to music with lyrics when work is manual, such as painting or raking.

SUGGESTIONS FOR SHOPPING AT THE MALL:

- Make a list before you go. If you know the store, list items according to where they're displayed. Your list will be like a treasure map, with a start and end mark.
- Park near the entrance to the store you will visit. If you are going to more than one store, park near the last store.
- Avoid going to the mall on Saturday mornings. When it is necessary to go, carefully prepare a plan of attack,

which Jennifer Myers calls "Surgical Strike Shopping." Go at a slow time, like a Tuesday. Figure out exactly where you need to go, limit your time at only one shop, and get in and out quickly. Limit your exposure to the sensory chaos.

CHAPTER 8

Seeking Sleep

For many adolescents with SPD, a good night's sleep would be a dream come true.

SPD often interferes with self-regulation, which affects our arousal level for falling asleep, sleeping soundly, and awakening refreshed. And what is necessary for developing self-regulation? Sleep!

Sleep is tune-up time. One function of sleep is allowing the adolescent body to perform internal work necessary for growth. Another function is to nourish the brain as it prunes unnecessary neural connections between brain cells and remaps important pathways.

Laurence Steinberg, PhD, among other experts, recommends that adolescents get eight and a half to nine and a half hours of sleep every night. That much sleep for most teens would be a dream come true. Most teenagers sleep seven or fewer hours. Homework and other occupations keep them up late, and school starts early. Also, in puberty, the adolescent brain may experience an internal clock shift, making teens inclined to go to sleep and wake up later than they did as children. (It's a pity that school schedules don't shift, too.) A good night's sleep is hard to find, and what is hard for typical teenagers may be even harder for teenagers with SPD.

Maturing teens become increasingly self-aware and able to determine their own sleep strategies. A sleep plan often involves exercise and wise food choices during the day and calming activities (away from TV, computers, and other electronic devices) in the evening. A plan may call for quiet music, or no sound whatsoever, or a place you can slip away to, like an SPD haven.

SENSORY PROCESSING DISORDER AND SLEEP

Types of sensory processing disorder that may disturb sleep:

- Tactile overresponsivity to touch sensations coming from pajamas, bed linens and blankets, someone else in the bed, or a lumpy mattress
- Auditory overresponsivity to sounds, such as house creaks, someone else's breathing, or rain, crickets, and traffic outside the window
- Visual overresponsivity to bedroom lights, streetlight glow coming through the windows, or even light-emitting diodes (LEDs) of computers and other electronic devices in standby mode
- Vestibular overresponsivity to passive, unexpected movement, as when a bedmate turns over and the mattress shifts
- Vestibular/proprioceptive craving for physical activity when your daily movement quota has not been met

Effects of disturbed sleep:

- Inefficient sensory feedback from ordinary sensations
- Ineffective self-control of emotions and desires

- Increased overall arousal level as the body tries to fight sleepiness, including higher levels of stress, anxiety, depression, irritability, and anger
- Irregularities in appetite, bowel movements, heart rate, and other functions of the interoceptive sense
- Decreased attention, memory, judgment, and problem-solving functions while taking tests, driving, and performing daily tasks

Falling asleep and staying asleep may be chronic problems for people with SPD. One reason is that street sounds and house sounds, which don't bother most other people, may be very irritating. Ember Walker says that when she tried to sleep as a teenager, "Even the bugs outside seemed like they all had their own megaphones." The breathing sounds of siblings or partners in the room may be intolerable.

Everyone has auditory preferences when it comes to sleep environments, and finding the just-right solution takes trial and error. Some prefer a soundless setting, favoring earplugs; others prefer listening to music at bedtime to combat annoying environmental sounds with pleasant background noise. Adding musical sounds to combat environmental noise may seem counterintuitive, but it often works well.

Many people with SPD opt for white noise. Composed of many frequencies with equal intensities, white noise masks and decreases sensitivity to environmental sounds to help people study, work, and sleep. It seems to raise the threshold for sounds so that many of them go unnoticed. Occupational therapists often recommend white noise machines.

Bugs outside the window may bother one person's ears, while a sensation of bugs on her skin may bother another. Not auditory sensations, but touch sensations are Shonda's "bugaboos." Her strategy is making sure the sheets and blankets are just right for her sensory needs.

I WAS A TEENAGE SHEET SNOB
SHONDA LUCAS

What is sleep like for a teenager with SPD? For me it was a mixed bag. Some nights, when I was in an underresponsive cycle, I was able to sleep for what felt like days, and I could fall asleep anywhere—just ask my sixth period geometry teacher: he'll tell you that I frequently fell asleep in my book at my desk! Sometimes it felt like I couldn't get enough sleep, no matter how early I went to bed or what time I got up.

There were also nights, though, when I couldn't fall asleep under any circumstance. It felt like I had bugs crawling on my skin, and if my blanket touched me, it actually hurt. Those nights, I would try anything to get to sleep. An antihistamine known for making you sleepy—that didn't help. A weighted blanket—nope, that made the bugs worse. A shower to get the buggy feeling off—no good. I would just have to suffer until the next night and hope to be so tired I could sleep through the buggy feeling.

Other nights, I felt almost manic. My brain would not shut off. This was especially true if I had danced as a cheerleader at a game, had a hard day at school, or worked that night. When I was overstimulated, there was no sleeping.

In my teens I became a "sheet snob." I had to have 100 percent cotton sheets, and the higher the thread count, the better. I slept under a heavy comforter even in the middle of a hot and sticky Florida summer. Friends and family would ask me if I wasn't burning up under the thick blankets—but heat didn't matter, as I needed the heaviness to be comfortable.

What helps me have fewer sleepless nights are soft sheets, a heavy blanket or two (or three), and a clear mind. Of course, that last one is hard to find sometimes.

A clear mind is often an important ingredient for a restful night. A weighted blanket, which can be calming, and a quiet room may not be enough. The best natural sedative may be having a trusted friend to help you talk through your worries and cares. Sometimes it's having someone right by your side who pays attention to you and holds you, such as your parent or loving partner.

Below, Jennifer McIlwee Myers tells us her solution for sleeping. Auditory overresponsivity kept her awake. When she investigated cognitive behavioral therapy (CBT) techniques to deal with anxiety, she was surprised to find that CBT also helps with physical issues of SPD.

RATIONAL THINKING LEADS TO PEACEFUL SLEEP
JENNIFER MCILWEE MYERS

The idea that a physical problem could be addressed through logic and psychological means is not one I would have guessed at, but there you are. You never know what you are going to find until you start moving.

Cognitive behavioral therapy is about replacing irrational beliefs ("the world is out to get me") with rational beliefs ("my situation at the moment may well suck but can most likely be improved").

I'd been practicing this a lot lately, and it came as a shock that after several months, coping with my sensory issues was becoming wa-a-ay easier than usual. For example, when a noise outside kept me from sleeping, it only kept me awake as long as it was going on, and no longer. I wasn't up for several hours because of a noise that had stopped after one hour.

The difference was in my conscious mental processing of the input. For as long as I could remember, if I was trying to sleep and people were making noise outside my window, I got really, really anxious and upset. Before I learned to practice CBT, I'd think things like, "Don't they know people need to sleep? People like that are always so rude, all the time. How many nights will they keep me from getting a good night's sleep? What if I can't sleep at all and can't get work done tomorrow? I might get in all kinds of trouble; but if I take a nap then I might get even less work done and get in even more trouble! These people are ruining my life because they are so inconsiderate! What mean bullies! My life could be ruined because people don't understand SPD and don't understand how sensitive my ears are! Oh, no, this is *terrible*. It's a completely *horrible* situation."

You get the idea. I was greatly disturbed not only by my neighbors, but also by my own thoughts. The fears I attached to my unpleasant sensory experience made me feel much worse than the actual sensory input did!

So when I switched my thinking around, I reduced the pain and stress. Mind you, I said, "reduced," not "obliterated totally." I was experiencing very real distress from sounds that really were unpleasant, and sometimes even sharply painful to me. But I wasn't doubling down via my own brain anymore—I cut the distress down to the basic sensory ouchiness of the situation, which was a big cut.

What does the "after" picture look like? Instead of the above, I was now thinking things like, "Well, this is annoying. It's not disastrous, but I sure don't like it. These folks have no idea of how sensitive I am. Oh, well, might as well distract myself. Okay, brain, cue up *Star Wars*, beginning with the opening text crawl . . . oh, darn, they're too loud for me to do that. Okay, let's try something easier: let's see how many of the classic *Doctor Who* serials I can name, starting with the Third Doctor: story 51, 'Spearhead from Space'; story 52, 'The Silurians'; story 53…"

Of course, sometimes I can't focus on anything other than the upsetting or painful input, but at least I don't let myself believe it's the end of the world if I miss a few hours of rest one night. And once the chatting friends outside have finally quieted down, to be able to sleep peacefully is beautiful, just beautiful.

Jenn's approach may help other teenagers with SPD. Adjusting sounds, sheets, bedtime, and so forth may help. For detailed suggestions, look at Lindsey Biel's *Sensory Processing Challenges* and her earlier book (coauthored with Nancy Peske), *Raising a Sensory Smart Child.*

GET IN TUNE TO GET SOME SLEEP

Peter Sullivan

Peter Sullivan is an environmental health researcher and the father of two sons who used to have serious sensory issues. Turning off household electronics helped them enormously. Peter writes about eliminating this new problem that interferes with everyone's life in the modern world. Learn more at www.clearlightventures.com.

Think of our nervous system as a stringed musical instrument. Sometimes it is too tight and "high-strung," other times too loose and "low-strung." We need to "tune" it for peak performance. When we are too high-strung, we seek harmonious environments and activities to calm us down. Harmony is another word for synchronization. Sensory activities and experiences that support and move us toward this state feel good.

All sensory experiences (sound, light, touch, etc.) are translated into electrical pulses or waves in our nervous systems and brains. They can get us in tune and keep us in tune or, if unsupportive, get us out of tune.

When we feel, we are paying attention to the state of these waves in our bodies. If we fail to pay attention to how our body feels, we not only miss opportunities to tune ourselves for optimal performance, but we may also remain in unhealthy environments in which it is impossible to stay synchronized.

Most people are not sensitive enough to feel the increasing, invisible environmental sources in our homes that can interfere with the nervous system. Some of these sources are:

- Cordless phone base stations
- Wi-Fi
- Baby monitors
- Circuit breakers controlling bedroom electrical outlets

The wireless radiation we commonly use to communicate is basically light that is a lower frequency than our eyes can see. Since wireless radiation is a form of light, leaving it on at night interferes with the production of melatonin (the hormone that controls sleep and wakefulness), just like leaving a light on in your bedroom would. If you could see this radiation, it would look like harsh flickering that overloads the nervous system.

Wireless radiation can penetrate through the body and cause us to feel out of sync and to become "de-tuned." As we become de-tuned, one of the primary functions that degrades is our senses! This creates a downward spiral of insensitivity to stressors that affect our health.

Unhealthy environments are a fundamental issue with SPD and autism. We have created spaces where it is hard to stay in harmony, and we are losing the sensitivity to override our body's feeling and instincts to leave. Staying in these environments requires great energy to keep synchronized and focused. It's no wonder that many children with SPD are irritable, exhausted, and sleepless at home and that some autistic children wander away from home or school.

Tell your family about this issue. To make your home—or at least your bedroom—more sensory friendly, turn off sources of constant wireless radiation, especially at night, for at least twelve hours. This simple step will restore sync, and you may feel less stressed and probably will sleep better.

Sound sleep is imperative for good health. When adolescents and young adults with SPD make sensible changes in their food choices, daily activities, bedtime routine, and bedroom environment, sleep improves and everything gets better.

COPING TIPS FOR COMMON SLEEPING CHALLENGES

WELL BEFORE BEDTIME:

- Get at least thirty minutes of whole-body exercise, preferably outdoors, every day and at least three hours before you plan to go to bed, to satisfy your sensory movement quota and to expose yourself to natural sunlight. If you can't get outdoors, jump on a mini-trampoline, walk on the treadmill, lift weights, or do some push-ups. Doing chores like laundry or vacuuming is a good way to engage in some heavy work activity, and it will help you sleep later.

- For two hours before going to sleep, avoid electronics—TVs, computers, phones, backlit devices, etc.—that can interfere with relaxation and suppress the release of melatonin, which brings on drowsiness.
- Turn off wireless devices in your bedroom and in the whole house, if possible.
- If possible, adjust the temperature in your bedroom to where it feels just right for sleeping.
- Avoid sugary snacks.
- If you are hungry toward bedtime, have a small turkey sandwich, a banana, or some low-sugar cereal with milk or yogurt.
- In the evening, avoid coffee and tea with caffeine, as well as alcohol, and even avoid too much water so you won't wake up needing to use the toilet.
- Avoid naps during the afternoon.
- If eating a full dinner makes you feel drowsy, don't snooze on the couch. Walk around the house, straighten your desk, or do something useful.
- If something is bothering you about school or friends or life, discuss it with your parents or a sibling, if possible. You may come up with solutions that will put your mind at ease so you won't toss and turn all night.

AT BEDTIME:

- Sleep in 100 percent cotton sheets with a high thread count, as well as cotton blankets and comforters.

- Go to bed at the same time every night to improve self-regulation.
- Relax with a calming activity:
  - Stroll around the block or do some slow and easy stretching.
  - Rock in a rocking chair.
  - Bounce lightly or roll on a therapy ball.
  - Take a warm bath.
  - Get a back rub or deep pressure.
  - Cuddle with someone (or a soft pillow).
  - Listen to quiet music from a regular, wired (not wireless) AM/FM radio, or put on a familiar, calming CD on continuous play. If one works really well, use it every time you lie down to sleep.
  - Read a real book or magazine (the kind with paper pages).
- Block out house or street sounds with earplugs, a whirring fan, a white noise machine, or static from your radio set imprecisely between stations.
- If light bothers you, block it out by wearing a sleep mask. Another idea to make the room completely dark is to tape something opaque, like aluminum foil, to your windows.
- If you must get up during the night, keep the lights low, use a flashlight, or switch on a night-light to get around safely.
- Sleep with a weighted blanket to help you know where your body ends.
- Breathe slowly and deeply, in through your nose, out through your mouth.

PART III

COPING WITH RELATIONSHIPS

CHAPTER 9

Living with SPD and Your Family

Sensory processing disorder is a family affair.

Families cope with the disorder in different ways, some more effectively than others. Their approach depends on their emotional, physical, and financial resources, on their family dynamics, and on their knowledge of SPD.

Relationships between parent and child may be rocky when SPD, which usually begins in infancy, goes unrecognized. I have a dear friend whose tactile overresponsivity when she was an infant caused her to recoil whenever her father reached to lift, cuddle, and kiss her. She arched her little back, stiffened, and wailed. Her father thought he must be hurting her. He would hastily put her down or hand her to his wife, the only person whose touch the baby girl could endure.

As she grew, and her sensory challenges increased, she and her father kept their distance, each believing that the other felt no affection. During her adolescence and young adulthood, their cold relationship became even icier. It didn't thaw until the gentleman was near death, many decades later. Tentatively, tearfully, they opened up and discussed their feelings of sad, bewildered estrangement from each other. Finally, they were able to hug and kiss.

Things could have been so different.

SPD complicates most relationships. Rough relationships may get rockier when children enter puberty, a particularly challenging stage of human development.

Unrecognized SPD causes still more complications. Uninformed parents, siblings, and grandparents may puzzle over an adolescent's unusual behavior. They may not know why the teenager can't move, talk, eat, sleep, wake up, wash up, get dressed, ride in the car, go places with the family, do homework, and behave as a tween, teen, and young adult "should"—especially when he or she is so smart!

Family members may be dismayed that kids with SPD are so different from themselves—and don't do things their way. A parent who enjoys carpentry and fixing things may scold a dyspraxic child who can't wield a hammer. A "touchy-feely" parent may insist on being physically demonstrative with an overresponsive child, even when the child pulls away. Frustrated parents may use a hit-or-miss approach to cope with their out-of-sync children, unwittingly making things worse. They may cry, get angry, or yell.

Remember Shonda Lucas helping her grandmother do laundry? Shonda's poor proprioceptive discrimination got in her way, and her grandmother thought she was acting like a "smart-ass." Several other adults recall discordant interactions that occurred because their parents, siblings, and relatives were ignorant of SPD. Here is an example:

MOST PARENTS DON'T GET THEIR KIDS WITH SPD
MARY ANN CONWAY

Most parents don't get their kids with SPD. When I was growing up, my mom didn't know how to handle me. She screamed at me a lot. Her loud pitch and tone of voice would hurt. I couldn't listen when she talked because her voice went right through me. I would hold my ears and yell, "Blah-blah-blah."

So if I didn't understand something, sometimes she would hit me (like that was going to do something). When I got home from school, I stayed away from her.

As a child and teenager, I was sent to my room a lot and would wonder why I was being punished. I would cry, because I didn't know what was happening to me. What did I do wrong? I had so much trouble learning the difference between wrong and right. So I would cry hard, put myself in a ball, rock, and bang my head against the wall. I wanted to find something to cut myself with to stop the pain.[1]

Our relationship is different now that I've been diagnosed. My mom doesn't remember any of what she did to me. Now we get along great.

As a mature adult, Mary Ann was diagnosed with mild autism, ADHD, central auditory processing disorder, and SPD. Her relationship with her mother is now a loving one, because they both have grown to understand her special needs and gifts.

Especially when a child has SPD, home should be a haven. But when an out-of-sync adolescent is clumsy, reacting to a scratchy shirt label, or desperate for some exercise—and just trying to survive—unenlightened parents may discipline with physical force, thinking that their son or daughter is deliberately misbehaving. Or parents may scream or hit because that is the treatment they received as children and the only response they know.

When all eyes and hands are on the kid who is easily aroused and can't calm down, it is no wonder that typically developing sib-

---

1   See chapter 3, "Coping and Hoping."

lings feel resentment that they are getting insufficient attention. Their responses may complicate family dynamics.

Sometimes they ignore or turn away from their embarrassing or frustrating sibling. Sometimes they look for ways to tease or goad the sensory brother or sister. Why? Because it is unfailingly easy and amazing how a little poke in the ribs or pat on the head can arouse the sibling's fast, intense, long-lasting, off-the-charts response.

Sometimes siblings are looking not for explosive reactions but for a calm home life. Assuming parental roles for the sibling whom they feel needs their protection, a conscientious brother or sister like this often grows up fast.

A SIBLING'S PERSPECTIVE
ABIGAYLE FISCH, JASON'S SISTER

Growing up with a sibling with SPD is no walk in the park. But I have slowly and surely started to appreciate being the sibling of a special-needs kid. It may sound cheesy, but I learned ways to take on the world that nobody else would be able to understand. Difficulties turned into capabilities.

For instance, I may have been "typical," but I was just a kid wanting some of the attention that my brother got lots of. I spent multiple meals by myself. It was difficult to be forgotten during dinnertime. But eating alone taught me to work independently. That trait has helped me to study and do well at school.

At school, I worried about Jason and felt very protective. It was hard to see him struggle, but still I was glad to be able to watch over him. Being protective is something I am very good at. I, now, am very patient and understanding of others; I have empathy that could only come from practicing it on my brother.

Weekends were not always so relaxing, with lots of Saturday afternoons waiting for my brother to calm down. My parents and I had to make sure he was comfortable before we could go out and do something. But waiting until we could get organized to have a family outing taught me how to entertain myself. That capability was crucial for my happiness as a kid and now that I'm a teenager.

When I was young, being his sister was not easy, but it was worth the hardship. Now that we're teenagers, we have come a long way. I'm proud of him—and of myself, too!

Universally, parents blame themselves when they can't meet everyone's needs and enjoy the family happiness they envisioned. Parents of children with SPD may be especially self-blaming.

The formidable task of parents, exhausted and exasperated as they may be, is to balance everyone's needs so that all family members get appropriate attention. They feel chronic sorrow—intense, recurring grief about what they perceive as a loss. They may think that were it not for their flawed genes, their imperfect parenting skills, their initial cluelessness about SPD, their unquestioning trust in uninformed professionals—then their child would suffer less and family life would be much, much easier.

PARENTS FEEL THE BLAME
MARLA ROTH-FISCH AND AARON FISCH, JASON'S PARENTS

We are now in the thrust of the teenage years. Our son, Jason, is fourteen, and we have been coping with his SPD since he was three. There is still so much to deal with:

- How to ease your child's sensory meltdowns
- Regulating the sunlight in your child's bedroom
- Figuring out the most comfortable, soft clothing
- Finding a food that doesn't cause your child to throw up
- Getting an occupational therapist that works well with your child
- The frustrating lack of understanding and knowledge about SPD
- Insurance issues
- Sleep deprivation
- Being there for your other child or children
- Feeling that you as the parent are to blame

As hard as it is for you as the parent, just think, it's a thousand times worse for your child. Children have to handle so many new sensory issues that come steamrolling their way as they get to their teens. There are hormone and physical changes, school stressors and social changes, and the "interaction within the family dynamic," which sometimes tips the balance of life inside the home. Fortunately, we (with the help of professionals) are able to give our son the help he needs. Providing the personal tools when kiddos are young certainly helps when they grow into teenagers.

SPD is nobody's fault. Successful parents are aware of that. Still, they may ache that their sons' and daughters' lives are so hard. Successful parents also are aware of how SPD affects everyone in the family. Despite the daily challenges, they appreciate family members' teamwork to help the out-of-sync child make progress.

Catering exclusively to the out-of-sync adolescent's needs, however, creates its own problems. Therefore, families get more in sync when they figure out how to balance everyone's needs. For instance, if the teen can't abide spicy food, perhaps everyone can start a meal with unseasoned food, and those who want extra pepper can add it to their own plates. If the teen needs vigorous sensory-motor experiences, the whole family will probably benefit from more physical activity when they incorporate it into daily life. If the teen needs quiet time and space, the family can plan how to give her a break and still have fun at the amusement park. Problem solving helps the adolescent participate in family life— and not be excused from joining in. (In chapter 12, "Treating SPD," read about Dr. Lucy Jane Miller's problem-solving method called A SECRET.)

The stories below exemplify how parents can respect and address their adolescents' sensory needs. Two mothers tell us how they have listened and learned to provide the sensory stimulation that is just right for their daughters—one a sensory craver, the other a sensory avoider.

I AM A SENSORY KID'S MOM
STEPHANIE J. WHITNEY, TYLER ANN'S MOTHER

Tyler Ann is a fourteen-year old sensory kid. To satisfy her need for intense vestibular and proprioceptive input, we have arranged our home and schedule so she can go through obstacle courses around the house, ride her bike before doing homework, and eat with the family while sitting on a therapy ball or an air-filled cushion.

As Tyler has grown she has become able to identify her own sensory needs and make her own adjustments. After a rough day, she comes home and heads straight for the outdoor trampoline. She rock climbs, rappels, jumps off waterfalls, is a star catcher for her high school softball team, competes in judo and karate, incessantly chews gum, still runs everywhere, and gets deep pressure whenever and however she can. She has a 4.0 grade point average, competes in the academic decathlon, is a member of many educational clubs and programs, and has tons of energy left over for family and friends. She is a true success story of how appropriate sensory input can make one individual unstoppable.

I look forward to seeing what Tyler will achieve in her lifetime. She says, "I am going to take over the world." Raising my daughter has been one of my most joyful and rewarding challenges.

ROLL RIGHT ON!
DEBRA EM WILSON, SHALEA'S MOTHER

It is a place where dreams come true, they say. After much planning, we were eager and delighted to be in the land of enchantment—but three rides into our Disneyland adventure, my daughter said, "Mom, will this day ever end?"

Shalea was frazzled. Her poor sensory system was on overload from the constant music and other sounds, the smells, the crowds, and the overzestful rides. (The gentle It's a Small World was about all she could take.)

I understood, as I was overwhelmed, too. You see, I was a sensory kid myself, and through my work with Shalea and other sensory teens, I'm always learning about how to cope with SPD.

I gave her a firm hug, known in the therapy world as deep pressure. The other kids went off to have a blast on the exhilarating rides. My daughter and I, on the other hand, found solace in a food court. We ordered crunchy pretzels to help calm our nerves and attempted to gather our senses in a quiet booth away from the masses. At the end of that long day, it was a relief to drive away.

That day, we learned with certainty that theme parks will never be satisfying environments for Shalea. Fortunately, she has other options and knows that the library or a peaceful lake is a more likely place where her dreams may come true.

A favorite quote of mine is from Dr. H. Stephen Glenn, an educator, mental health advocate, and family psychologist, whose personal school challenges included dyslexia, ADHD, and, I suspect, SPD. Dr. Glenn tells audiences, "My fourth grade teacher said to me that I will always be a round peg in a square hole, and my job was to organize things so rolling is an advantage."

Isn't that what we hope our teens can do for themselves? As a parent of a sensory teen, I marvel at how my daughter has figured out how to organize herself in a world that is often disorganized and unpredictable. She's on a roll—as are all our sensory teens. With understanding and support, rolling can be an advantage, and sometimes that means to roll right on past theme parks. Just keep on driving!

How sweet it is when teenagers grow up enough to figure out what works for them, and when the family learns to roll right along as a synchronized team. This evolution can be transformative. (See the following box.)

TUNING IN TO SPD

Minna Loketch Fischer

Minna has a background in mental health counseling and is currently completing her Doctorate in Psychology at Hofstra University. Her primary clinical focus is on pediatric health and neuropsychology.

Teenagers and adults with SPD often describe the isolation they feel from their family and friends. By learning how to communicate with one another, those with SPD and their loved ones can avoid the negative effects SPD can have on relationships.

Adolescence itself is an age of natural tension between parents and children. Parents and teens are at completely different stages of life; they see things in an entirely different way. When children talk to parents and parents talk to children, they may have no idea what each other is saying, and that disconnection can be incredibly frustrating for both.

An issue like SPD, ADHD, or anxiety disorder (to name a few) just adds another aspect of contention and misunderstanding. Such issues are not clearly visible to the naked eye and are therefore harder to understand and have empathy for. It is easier to empathize with someone who has a huge, open gash across his face because you can see it and imagine what it might feel like. However, like a toothache or a headache, SPD is not easily visible, and it's harder to imagine the pain that the sufferer is going through.

Finding a way to communicate so each side can understand the other is necessary to ease the tension and frustration. How can this possibly be done?

Successful communication is best explained by using radio technology as an analogy. There are radio waves traveling through the air, which is a "language" our brain and ears can't understand. However, when you tune in to the right station, the radio can intercept the waves and transform the broadcast into something we can hear and understand.

Teenagers and parents send out radio waves to each other, but often both of them are tuned to the wrong station. The kids can understand only their own waves, and the parents can understand only what they send out. To be on the same wavelength—to have a functional, positive, and productive relationship—we must learn to send out the correct waves, or we have to learn to change our stations. I think a combination of both can be done, in three steps.

Step One: Changing Your Radio Waves

The first step is understanding what message you are trying to get across. Once you do that, you can begin to convert the message so that it can be understood. This is not easy; it requires introspection and self-understanding. Sometimes we want to get a message across to someone, but we're not really sure what our actual message is.

Let's put ourselves in an adolescent's shoes. Do you really want to say, "I hate you, you never understand me, this shirt is so itchy and I refuse to wear it, and I don't like your style, anyhow"? Or is the real message that you are trying to get across, "I feel uncomfortable in itchy sweaters, and when you force me to wear them, I feel unloved and not cared for and unimportant"? Now, wearing the parent's shoes, what are you trying to get across? Is it, "You are crazy and unmanageable, just wear the dumb sweater"?

Or is it really, "I have no idea what you are going through. I can't understand it, and I don't know how to handle this, so please just wear the sweater and stop making me feel like I don't know how to be a good parent."

Once you understand the message, you can begin to change the radio waves into a language that the receiver might understand—not only by rephrasing the message as we did above, so that the other person can really hear what you are saying, but also by helping that person to empathize. I believe that everyone can understand SPD if it's put into a language they can tune in to on the right station.

Step Two: Changing Your Station

We all have the same basic sensory systems, yet not all input is experienced in the same way by everyone. We need to get another person's sensory experience in sync with our radio waves so we can begin to receive it and understand it.

Try to find common ground so that you're on the right station to hear what your loved one is trying to tell you. Ask yourself, "What sensory stimulus makes me nuts?"

For example, many people are bothered by the sound of nails scratching on a blackboard. Imagine the feeling you get when that happens. Do you feel shivers, dread, shortness of breath, and discomfort?

Now transport those feelings to the particular sensory issues that your loved one with SPD has. Imagine having that feeling of dread every time you get dressed, are under fluorescent lights, or when there are too many moving things in your visual field. Imagine the shivers when someone taps you on the shoulder or when the clock is ticking in the background.

Understanding how the person feels on a day-to-day basis can make it clear why some people have such a hard time doing things or being in situations that seem to come so easily to you. Realizing that the uncomfortable response you have to one sensory stimulus can also apply to a different stimulus will help you feel empathy.

This kind of communication can help adolescents and parents understand one another's language and issues that have been so foreign to them.

Step Three: Investing

The last step in creating more positive relationships is investing. A good businessperson goes through a series of steps when investing his or her money. Our relationships are something worth investing in so we won't be so frustrated. A good businessperson starts with research.

Learn as much as you can about your loved one's sensory struggles. Learn about his or her unique strengths and perspectives in life. And learn as much as you can about yourself.

A good businessperson perseveres. When the portfolio drops, it doesn't mean you need to quit. When the difficult days come, persevere. Check your stocks, engage in communication, and adjust your behavior and thoughts as needed.

In addition, a good businessperson never does things alone. Consult with experts in the field, OTs, psychologists, other parents, and teachers. Every relationship requires maintenance, attention, and work, and in the end, it is one of the greatest investments we can make in both our own and our child's life.

Successfully tuning in to one another hugely benefits family relationships. When sensory challenges are addressed, parents and teens are better equipped to enjoy a more relaxed family life—and in-sync relationships at home pave the way for in-sync relationships out in the big world.

COPING TIPS FOR COMMON CHALLENGES WITH FAMILY RELATIONSHIPS

Research shows that the quality and quantity of time that teenagers and parents (especially mothers) spend together improves emotional well-being, social behavior, and even math scores! Everyone needs to feel a sense of belonging, and belonging begins at home.

• Carve out daily or weekly times in your schedules for sensory activities you all can enjoy. If car trips or state fairs delight some of you and distress others, look for neutral pursuits that bring you together. Here are a few ideas for at-home activities:
  • Preparing food
  • Housekeeping
  • Washing the car
  • Gardening
  • Walking, hiking, biking, and other outdoor activities
  • Walking the dog
  • Doing errands
  • Having a pillow fight
  • Watching a movie, perhaps a comedy to get you all laughing together
  • Writing postcards to friends and relatives
  • Playing board games or doing jigsaw puzzles

- Organizing photographs and designing scrapbooks
- Having a "cleanup blitz." (Find cleanup blitz cards on the Internet, or make your own.) This is where you work simultaneously and briefly to tidy up the house. Chores are more fun when the whole family is involved, plus they provide proprioceptive input, called "heavy work activity," that greatly benefits everyone with SPD.
- Get family therapy to learn how to relate better with one another.
- Consider attending religious services together.
- As a family unit, become "compassionate collectors." A socially active enterprise like this has innumerable benefits for the family and the community. Not only does this work encourage mindfulness of others, but it also nourishes the sensory systems and develops praxis. Just think of all the ideation, planning, and execution involved in:
  - Growing and/or preparing food to bring to a shelter for homeless people
  - Collecting clothes, toiletries and cosmetics, and canned and packaged food, and then sorting, boxing, lifting, and carrying the items to a shelter
  - Asking neighbors for furniture and housewares, sports equipment, musical instruments, books, and other useful items to donate to schools or communities where these items are appreciated

CHAPTER 10

Making Friends

Envision yourself as a teenager with sensory overresponsivity, going to a birthday party with a new friend from school. This is a nice opportunity for you to get to know this person who shares some common interests. But once you get to the party, you feel overwhelmed by sensations, and coping with them is all you can do.

Imagine that it sounds as if other people are hollering and guffawing, not speaking in conversational tones. They chomp noisily on celery and chips. Their forks screech against their plates and teeth. They make sudden gestures, plop themselves down, jump up, move about, and bump into you.

The doorbell rings shrilly, the dog barks, and in comes the pizza delivery man. To the other partygoers, Huzzah! To you, Horrors! Your nose prickles from the smell of tomato sauce and garlic. Others eat it with gusto; you meet it with disgust.

The lightbulbs are too bright, and you can hear them buzz. Then someone dims the lights—ah, that's a visual and auditory relief—until the flickering birthday candles and that awful "Happy Birthday" song load on more pain.

Meanwhile, your shirt, which you chose with such care, can't truly have been made from the finest pima cotton, as the label (the one you cut out) said. The shirt must have been made from porcupine quills. Porcupine quills and sandpaper.

Your feet are Not OK. The dress-up shoes you rarely wear because they hurt . . . hurt. Your imprisoned toes can sense every stitch in the leather. They want to get out; they want flip-flops. They want to go home.

Nothing is OK.

You take a deep breath and try to attend to what this nice, new, interesting person is saying to you. But, given your sensory overload, how is that possible? Why didn't you stay home, under the covers?!

While surviving in the social world can *seem* impossible, surviving without other people *is* impossible. People need people. Teenagers are at the developmental stage when they rely less on their families for company and counsel and seek people their own age. Just as fledglings grow the feathers needed to fly, typical teenagers gradually acquire the physical and social abilities needed to venture forth and find their place and purpose in the world.

But these abilities may be latent in adolescents who, as children, avoided any physical or social situation that made them feel uncomfortable or awkward. They may have preferred playing a video game alone in their room over shooting baskets with neighborhood kids at the playground. As they grew, they may have missed opportunities to practice having casual conversations, sharing fun times, and developing enduring friendships.

THOSE AWKWARD YEARS
PAUL BALIUS

I never had a close friend growing up. This is an unfortunate casualty of sensory issues. Growing up it was important to keep my secret safe. I longed to be with others but was forced to be a loner. It was better to be a loner than to be exposed for how I really was. It's often too embarrassing to explain to people about my condition, as they just cannot grasp it.

As a teenager, the condition was even worse as I tried to fit in and work my way through those awkward years. The more I tried to fit in, the more I felt alienated from the world. It was like I had landed on another planet, and I looked like the aliens but was a different creature altogether. So the easiest solution was to avoid having friends.

Life as a teenager with SPD can be precarious. Contending with bullies is painful and exhausting. Complaining about sensory problems doesn't win friends. Regrettably, many would-be friends don't understand that the teenager with SPD doesn't want to go to a movie because the sounds in the theater hurt, or to a football game because the lights and noise and crowds cause confusion and anxiety. It's a joy to find a few true, enduring friends who know and accept the person, as is.

BULLIED THEN, BETTER NOW
NICOLE WOLSKE

Around the time I turned thirteen, my parents split up, and that was very hard for me. Also, I became a woman and wasn't too sure how to deal with that. I knew I liked guys, but I wasn't as boy crazy as most girls.

I was bullied a lot because of my SPD and called "weird" all the time. It was hurtful because I didn't have friends, and the ones I thought were my friends would one day be my friend and the next day pick on me. Gym time was a nightmare because my gym teacher would always tell me to stop being afraid of the ball, but she didn't realize I had SPD.

Around eighth grade, I had finished my occupational therapy sessions. The OTs felt I was ready to be on my own and help myself.

Then I started high school. I knew mentally I was smart but also emotionally much younger acting than everyone else. As my father would always tell me, I was fifteen going on twelve. While other girls were excited about boys, I was more interested in school and doing well. Yes, I liked guys, but I always got turned down.

I had a very hard time making friends in high school and trying to relate to other teens because I was not near their level emotionally. Guys were another story because I was the small girl with the big, thick glasses, which did not appeal to anyone. When I did meet guys who liked me, they ended up being jerks and breaking my heart. While other teen girls were thinking of sex, that word actually scared me because I was afraid of the pain that comes with your first time.

Little by little, I did grow emotionally. After high school I made friends in college. I am in several Facebook groups that help a lot. I still want to find other young adults like me who understand what I go through.

After reading many books about SPD, I have come to a wonderful decision. I am going to get my master's in occupational therapy and specialize in sensory integration. I feel I would be a great force to work with because I can relate to all children who have this disorder. Discovering SPD was very emotional for me, and I am glad I finally figured it out.

Paul and Nicole exemplify adults who made it through their lonely adolescence. Now with their feet on the ground, they have become participants in the world.

Meanwhile, other writers still feel at sea in social situations. SPD affected their physical, psychological, and social development during their formative years.

SLOWLY LEARNING TO SWIM
JOANNA LEES

My formative years could be summed up in one word: flailing. Imagine a very unsteady girl trying to learn to swim, one foot just barely touching the bottom of the pool, arms and legs frantically waving and kicking while she tries to stay afloat, or at least keep her head above water. Now imagine that girl waving and kicking not just in the water, but out of it, and you have the picture.

I was homeschooled. While activities such as 4-H provided some social exposure, I was largely isolated from others my own age. I missed the day-to-day interactions that help with social and emotional development. Sadly, my home environment was a pretty dysfunctional place and not much help. I was given little guidance on how to behave in public or in private. At fourteen, when I reentered public school, I found myself completely lost, caught in a sea of hormones and social interactions I had absolutely no idea how to navigate.

Adolescence is a crummy time to learn skills that usually develop in early childhood. I was hopelessly out of touch with my own unspoken, ungainly signals, and I had even less understanding of others' body language and facial expressions. Thus, instead of reaching out, I retreated into myself. I had always sought refuge in books and, when I could get it (rarely in our household), TV and the Internet. Now, confronted by an environment I couldn't interpret, I withdrew even further.

My mother read The Out-of-Sync Child when I was about fifteen. The general reaction at home was, "Good heavens, this explains everything." Now we knew (to some degree) why I flailed around, why I couldn't keep track of my arms and legs, why I lost my mind on long car trips, why I had to sit at one specific place at the dinner table—why I drove everyone crazy (and vice versa!). However, I was mostly left to my own devices when it came to managing my symptoms. My parents and siblings often tried to be accommodating, letting me grab hold of them when I was overwhelmed by crowds, letting me sit where I needed to sit, and so on. Beyond that, the message was, "We've done our part— why aren't you 'normal' yet?"

"Normal" was something I just couldn't reach—physically, emotionally, or socially. My inability to pick up on social cues, coupled with my mental and emotional dysfunction, created a feedback loop that nearly drowned me. By the time information filtered through my nervous system to my skewed thought processes, it was mostly just noise. I interacted very little with classmates and teachers. Outside of marching band and a semester working crew for the musical, my extracurriculars were nonexistent.

College was the same story. I developed an addiction to the Internet. When I wasn't in class, I was on the computer. Social events came rarely, sometimes with weeks in between. I never went to parties, never drank, and never did drugs. However, my "clean living" was, again, due as much to avoidance and lack of opportunity as anything else. I didn't go to drinking parties because I didn't go to any parties. I felt like I needed a direct invitation, a confirmed instance of permission, before I could participate. Anything beyond showing up and taking notes in class was too much to contemplate. My few attempts to make social connections were so clumsy and mishandled that I made little progress. The flailing was still there, just less obvious on the outside.

I was addicted to the Internet because it provided a sense of interaction without the dangers of face-to-face contact. I didn't have to worry about stepping on toes or tripping over the furniture or making eye contact or getting pushed or jostled in the crowd. I didn't have to worry about making a fool of myself by standing too close or talking too loud. The computer, TV, and books (writing as well as reading them) became my hiding place, a source of emotional junk food. If I couldn't stop the flailing, I reasoned, I would just stay inside where it couldn't get in the way. My attitude toward myself was, "I can't take you anywhere."

Eventually I joined a church group on campus, much in the way I had joined the marching band in high school. I showed up enough times that I felt safe interacting on a basic level. I rarely had contact with other members outside of group events. As with my bandmates, the moment I graduated I lost touch. Because I couldn't establish real personal connections, as soon as the situation changed, it was like either I or they had fallen off the face of the earth.

While I've learned to deal with a lot of the baggage and dysfunction that have always weighed me down, the flailing is still there and likely always will be. I still talk with my arms and speak in sounds instead of words when I get excited. I still find bruises that can only be explained by assuming I didn't notice the last time I ran into the furniture. It's still a challenge to interact in a way that would be considered "normal."

What progress I have made has been largely through conscious choice with the help of a close friend and mentor. I still feel like I need permission to join in with others. I still have to watch that I don't explode in a blast of enthusiasm and flail myself right back out. I will probably always feel safer with a book than with a person. But at least by this time, I have some understanding why. It's taken most of my young life and a lot of work, but I am, slowly, beginning to learn to swim.

SPD overwhelms Joanna. Fortunately, she has found a harbor, living with her godmother who also has sensory issues and really understands. She is planning to take swimming lessons. The tide may soon turn for this hopeful young woman.

Given how powerful sensory input, especially auditory stimulation, can be, it's no wonder conversations are often very challenging. (See the following box.) Involving most senses, a conversation can trigger a fight, flight, freeze, or fright response for many individuals with SPD, particularly teens. Their neurological system

can scream, "Leave me alone! Don't hurt me!" They don't want to
talk away—they just want to walk away.

HOW SPD MAY AFFECT CONVERSATIONS

- Tactile overresponsivity may cause worry (sometimes
  subconscious) that the person you are talking to will
  touch you unexpectedly.
- Inefficient auditory discrimination may make it hard
  to understand what another person is saying.
- Poor proprioception may interfere with positioning
  your tongue and lips correctly to articulate your words
  well.
- An out-of-sync vestibular sense may make it hard to
  stand still.
- Another person's scent may insult your olfactory
  sense.
- Animated facial expressions may confuse you visually.
- With anxiety about all these realities and possibilities,
  your interoceptive sense (the sense of internal organs)
  can get out of sync, and your stomach may be upset.
  You may want to throw up your hands and leave, or
  just throw up.

Next, several young people with SPD describe how inarticulate
they become in conversations. Expressing their feelings is easy
when they write or type but difficult when they are trying to communicate face-to-face.

FEELING SAFE IN ONE'S OWN SKIN
CHLOE ROTHSCHILD

Accumulated sensory input, especially noise, can be way too much to handle, which is why I often isolate myself in my room with the door shut. But because I live in a neurotypical world, over the years I have forced myself to participate in activities and go places, at least for a short time, because I cannot be alone forever. But I suffer from this later, and then I have to deal with a feeling of overload in me and my body.

Combine my numerous sensory sensitivities with social anxiety and simply not knowing what to say to people—it can be a nightmare. And I know at times people try to help me by talking to me, but this makes my overload worse. Give me a break! Write down what you want to say, and allow me to do the same.

Being around other people for prolonged lengths of time can be hard. I often don't engage with people in conversations. Sometimes I wonder how much of this is because I lack so many social skills or because of the great sensory overload that interacting causes. I bet this is why engaging with peers can be so hard, since I live in almost constant overload! Can you imagine?

And then someone expects you to have a conversation? Forget about it!

TELL ME, COULD YOU SPEAK?
LYDIA WAYMAN

At one point, when my sensory processing was more out of sync than ever, I even struggled to understand what people were saying to me. I used to find great comfort in the Food Network (I know, it's funny, for the girl who won't touch most foods), but I grew frustrated with the intense focus I needed to process the words that felt like they flew by at warp speed. I have always loved church, or at least the idea of church, but I couldn't bear the lights and music and motion of the people.

Sometimes I experience synesthesia, or the mixing of sensory input. For example, I've been known to say, "Those lights are hurting my ears." It may sound outlandish, but this phenomenon is very real and very confusing.

When things get entirely too overwhelming and out of sensory sync, even after a long day with a lot of processing involved, my speech shuts down on me. This always surprises people. But if you were seeing sounds and feeling lights, if you couldn't understand what was being said to you, if you felt like a bolt of electricity was going through your brain, tell me, could you speak?

Whereas some teens with SPD are uncomfortable in social situations, others are eager to mingle. They like to be with other people their age, but everyone else talks too loudly and too fast.

I HAVE A LOT TO SAY
KEVIN LARSON

Auditory oversensitivity makes social gatherings really hard. When people are too loud or crazy, I get overwhelmed and feel like I'm being attacked. At youth group meetings, which are pretty noisy, I usually give up trying to talk to the other kids. And then people look at me like I'm stupid. And I'm not.

It's frustrating, because the kids usually talk so fast and loud that by the time I think of something to say, they've moved on and my comments no longer fit. I feel irrelevant although I have a lot to say. I usually end up sitting with the grown-ups instead. Only adults listen well to my ideas.

In one way, maturing makes matters worse. Social situations are so much more complex. Now it's not about just kicking a ball around or racing to win, not about just hearing what other people say, but about reading them and figuring out what they really mean and expect. Having autism, I don't feel like I *have* to fit in. But it sure would make things easier.

As I get older, people expect more of me socially. And I'm more self-conscious now that I'm fifteen. I can see it in people's eyes that some of them think I'm weird. And that hurts. A lot.

However, maturing also does help to some degree. Growing up, I have had many positions of leadership in my community, across plenty of different fields, and I believe my social skills are strengthening. I have learned to work as part of a team, and that the best leader is the best listener. I have become better at interpreting what people really mean. I can't change how people act, although I can try to have a positive influence on them. I'm open to more possibilities for friendship than ever.

Adolescents with SPD may be more socially successful in a sensory-friendly environment. They welcome extra time so they can think, speak, and respond, and sufficient space so they don't feel pushed or stifled.

THE GIFT OF TIME AND SPACE
LAURIE APPEL

It's funny—growing up, as much as I wanted to hide from the world, I often found myself to be the center of attention because of my quirky behaviors. I remember climbing a tree, then spending hours crying because I was too afraid to climb down, while the entire neighborhood gathered to watch.

Getting stuck while crossing a stream, poised to go down a slide, scaling a jungle gym, or standing on the diving board at the pool were all repeats of the same story, with my gravitational insecurity[1] kicking in and me just trying not to be noticed.

I've developed some strategies that are more socially appropriate than covering my ears and screaming or throwing things and slamming doors. In conversations, I've developed practices like taking a deep, calming breath as I bring my eyes up and to the left to access the part of my brain needed to answer a question. I keep my body open so the person I'm in conversation with knows that I am still present and engaged. This practice helps me feel safe, so that I can filter and process what's important and respond to the sensory input bombarding me.

The main way that others can support people with SPD is to give us time and space. Then we can be seen, heard, and understood for who we are.

Socially, things may improve as teenagers mature and become more self-aware of their differences, their desires, and their decisions about whom to befriend, what to believe, and how to "be" in the world. The story below points out that it helps greatly to develop a keen interest in a topic or activity and to seek out others who love it, too.

I AM HERE
ZACHARY PROSSICK-BROWN

SPD plays into many aspects of my personality. I have trouble thinking clearly when I am overstimulated by noises or when I am dealing with too many people at once. I am introverted, reserved, and shy. I am not

---

1   Gravitational insecurity is extreme fear and anxiety about falling.

introverted, reserved, and shy because I have SPD, but it probably makes me more so. SPD exacerbates other idiosyncrasies of someone's personality.

Most of my adolescence was spent by myself. I was very isolated and alienated from other people. SPD was definitely a major reason for that. It affects my self-esteem. I have always had issues with depression. How I have felt about myself has led me to make some bad decisions. It took me a long time, but I have learned that moods pass. Feeling very happy passes, as does feeling very sad. I try to keep myself busy and involved with things in my life.

I did not like school. When I was in high school and college, I used to smoke, a lot. In college I had very bad social anxiety. Because of this I started drinking, a lot. Now I don't need to smoke and drink to have friends. I feel like I have my own life to take care of.

In the last few years I have grown more as a person than I did when I attended college. I have real relationships with people. I have friends. People I meet are interested in me. I am interested in other people.

I have always loved making art and got my bachelor's degree in fine art. I volunteer at a community center where artists with disabilities go and work on art. The majority of my friends are involved with art in one way or another. Having an identity among other people is very important to me. It helps me feel like I matter, that I am here. For a very long time I didn't really feel like I was here, or that my existence mattered very much. Now I try to be a positive influence in my friends' lives. They are very important to me.

Once young people with sensory challenges connect with others around them, SPD does not preclude friendships. Indeed, it may enhance them. An "aha" moment often occurs when it becomes abundantly clear that friendship doesn't depend on ball skills, clothing preferences, or hairstyle. Rather, it depends on deeper qualities, such as kindness, compassion, and creativity. Coming to accept—and even embrace—SPD is an important step along the way to forming close friendships with diverse collections of true friends who appreciate one another for who they are.

MY SPD IS AN ASSET
ANNETTE HIMMELREICH

When I was growing up, making friends was easy because I was always the entertainment in the room. I jumped right in and introduced myself with some sort of joke. I have a very eclectic sense of humor. I learned to be mindful that not everyone wants a hug. I tend to hug people—this is my tactile craving—and I know that some of the overresponsive types out there may not like that.

Another big issue in making friends is that some can get overwhelmed with my talkative and entertaining-type personality. As I grew, I learned to develop several groups of friends, each with a different set of shared interests. Then I don't overwhelm any one group. My friends, like my humor, are very eclectic!

Close friends know about my SPD now. Some think my sensory issues are superhero abilities, in a way. For instance, I can hear even a whisper by aiming my big left ear, my "Lucky Fin," toward someone and can repeat what was said. My friends are always so impressed! Some friends come to me and ask questions concerning people they care about who have been diagnosed with SPD, and it's an honor to help them. My SPD is an asset in many relationships.

FRIEND COLLECTOR
RACHEL S. SCHNEIDER

For all my quirks and differences, I never had trouble making friends. I gravitated toward kids who were kind, imaginative, engaging, and embracing without necessarily knowing why. The kids I didn't want to spend time with just rubbed me the wrong way.

Back in my teens, my "anxiety disorder" (undiagnosed SPD) kept me at a distance. It kept me from parties and from hanging out at the marina next to my school, where other teens, with cigarettes at the edge of their lips, scowled and scoffed at passersby.

I looked for the sensitive homebodies, the challenging smarties, the people on the fringe, and befriended them. I trusted that these individuals would see me, all of me, and not just the bits of me that didn't fit the ideal teenage mold.

I understood that I had limitations, even if I didn't know what to call them. I compensated for what I couldn't do with what I could do—I could read people, feel their energy, and intervene to support their needs. I was the go-to for advice—a layman therapist who held sessions in the stairway when anyone burst into hormonally induced tears in the middle of English class. Teachers would often look my way and give me a nod, almost as if to say, "All right, kid, go and work your magic, go and save your friend," and within minutes we'd be back in the brightly lit classroom, heads down in *Hamlet*.

I have thought of myself as the Friend Collector since college. I always have a diverse group of friends. I bring two or three people from each area of my life with me as I move into the future: the clearheaded and thoughtful high school best friend, the quiet and loyal college friend, the wise "older sister" from work, the extended grad school family, the brilliant friend-of-a-friend, the hilarious camp friends. I have maybe a dozen close friends from all facets of my world. Together, they form a rich tapestry of qualities and values. Each person is distinct, and each reminds me of who I was when we met and how far I've come in my life.

My friends accept me and my SPD without reservation. They celebrate my contributions to their lives as I celebrate what they bring to mine. They work to ensure that I don't have to cross the thresholds of any sensory boundaries, unless, of course, that's something I'm looking to do, and then they're extended "handlers,"[2] trained—purely by knowing me—in helping me find a way to cope with my challenges, stay strong, and be positive. They're there for me, and in turn, I am here for them.

SPD SOCIAL LIVES—IT'S NO OXYMORON!

Daniel Travis

Why do we, the many teenagers and young adults with SPD, have such great difficulty finding friends?

Friendships are demanding. We have to get lucky and find a peer or two who understand us. They may have the same problems we face, have other difficulties that make them sympathetic to our struggles, have a sibling with issues similar to ours, or simply have a good heart and be open to all types of people.

As this kind of friend is rare, we struggle to find anyone outside our families with whom we feel comfortable. Also, finding an understanding peer may not lead to a friendship, since the person may share none of our interests or may have a voice, scent, or other physical attribute that offends our delicate systems.

---

2 "Handler" is Rachel's term for someone who helps a person with SPD to interact better with the world.

Of course, if we are in an environment that constantly triggers fight-or-flight responses, how are we ever going to care about finding friends? Our brains tell us we're in a near-death situation, and we go through our lives just trying to survive. Friends? What are those? We just want to make it back home in one piece!

So where can we find people who are more likely—though not guaranteed—to love and understand us? Yes, you guessed it, back home. Those of us with SPD spend more time with our families than with peers, especially if family members are caring and accepting and try not to push our buttons.

There is power in being content with spending time with our families. We still learn about the balance of relationships, the intricacies of social interaction, and other facets of the world around us. Sure, while our self-confidence may not grow as quickly, and we may not be as well prepared for adulthood, we still benefit greatly from having tight-knit family bonds. While SPD teens and young adults may have some of the worst friendship track records, many of us compensate by having much better relationships with our parents and siblings than others.

Does this mean we should be content in having no friends? Definitely not! Friendships are some of the best support out there, and perhaps the best form of therapy ever. True friends have your back and will understand you, no matter what. They are the gateway to increasing your self-esteem and sense of peace with the world at large.

"Sounds great," you may say. "But I can never make or keep friends. I can't stand to be around other people, and other people can't stand to be around me."

Fear not! You can change the game with three simple
steps:

1. Avoid sensory triggers. If a crowd will make you defensive and a roller coaster will make you seasick,
   don't look for friends at a bar or amusement park.
2. Seek enjoyable sensory input that helps you focus and
   feel balanced.
3. See an OT and add into your life various SI techniques that can rewire your nervous system.

Taking these steps to develop a sensory lifestyle, now
you may be ready to start seeking friendships. It may take
you months, or years. However long it takes, you will definitely be glad you did it.

Take it from someone who had no friends and spent all
day, every day, in his room. Take it from someone who
now has a budding social life and has been busier and more
in touch with his world than ever before. I write books,
produce and manage websites, play recreational hockey,
take leading roles in the office, volunteer my spare time,
attend frequent fellowship meetings, and spend my weeks
surrounded by amazing friends.

An SPD social life is no oxymoron! Take it from someone whose life has never been better. Please, take it from
me—and believe it!

Surely, SPD can make it hard to approach others, hold conversations, learn about other people's interests, and develop lasting

friendships. Getting out there and getting in sync with others may take lots of purposeful practice for young people with SPD. It helps when young people know that their family thinks they're great and loves them, no matter what. It helps to have frequent, positive interactions with family members in order to figure out what's fun and safe to do with peers, especially when parents aren't looking. It also helps to pay attention to other people's social customs and sensory preferences, not just our own. This all takes resolve and work—and the reward of a satisfying social life is worth all the effort.

COPING TIPS FOR COMMON SOCIALIZING CHALLENGES

IF YOU ARE IN A SOCIAL SITUATION AND NEED AN ESCAPE:

- Head to the bathroom. It will be quiet (unless it has a noisy hand dryer—best to scout it out in advance!).
- Use your phone or tablet—with restraint. It's easy to resort to reading text messages or e-mail so you can take a break from the stimuli around you, but don't linger over the device. You are there to be friendly. The big rule is not to use technological devices during times of relationship building, such as during dinner or when others seek your attention.

TO STICK WITH A CONVERSATION, EVEN IF YOU WOULD RATHER ESCAPE:

- Breathe deeply.
- Try to keep eye contact, but if it is too taxing, move your eyes up and to the left, slightly above the other person's head.

• Stand tall and wide. Keep your feet pointed toward
  the person to show you are present and engaged. Feet
  pointed toward the door are a giveaway that you would
  rather be elsewhere.

OTHER TIPS:

• Tell the people who really need to know about your
  SPD. For instance, if going to a concert will hurt your
  ears, explain to your friend that your overresponsivity
  is a physical problem, and you can't help it.

• If someone in particular pulls your sensory triggers,
  limit or eliminate that relationship. You have every
  right to pick and choose friends who are constructive,
  not destructive, in your life.

• If you tend to be overly effusive and to seek physical
  contact, try to restrain your hugs and enthusiasm,
  which may overwhelm friends.

• Develop friendships with more than one or two people. Concentrating on one person limits both of you.

• Develop friendships based on common interests. Is
  art, music, dancing, riding horses, or jumping over
  waterfalls your favorite activity? Find others who
  share your passion, meet in a public place at first, and
  if you are compatible, start a regular group.

CHAPTER 11

Dating, Kissing, and Beyond

If conversing can be confusing, dating can be daunting. Nonetheless, as the first-person accounts in this chapter illustrate, romance and true love do happen and can be as wonderful and enjoyable for people with SPD as they can be for everyone else.

Before we get to happily-ever-after, we'll hear the accounts of several adults reflecting on their teenage dating experiences, or lack thereof. One problem that distresses some teenagers with SPD is their conviction that they are unlovable. They may worry that their bodies will behave in inappropriate ways at any time and especially at the wrong time. They may regret that their particular sensory requirements make life difficult for people they want to be near. They may feel deeply that they do not deserve love. Indeed, some may strive all their lives for reassurance that they are lovable—reassurance that most neurotypicals take for granted.

I GET THE MESSAGE
BOB ARGUE

Dating flat-out never happened. I was the lowest anyone could possibly be in the social order in high school. I never went to the prom, because nobody wanted to go out with me. I've given up on dating. After many women telling me that I'm inferior to them, I get the message: nobody wants me.

In the stories below, you'll see how out-of-sync tactile, proprioceptive, vestibular, visual, auditory, olfactory, gustatory, and interoceptive systems can make dating—and particularly kissing—an ordeal.

THE OCCASIONAL KISS
JOANNA LEES

My dating history has been anything but typical. My only post-high-school relationship lasted six months. Physical intimacy is conspicuously absent from my experience. Again, my inability to establish connections and my discomfort in the presence of others combined for a lethal effect on my "love" life. I am a virgin.

There were a few high points during my high school years, but they tended to be islands, few and far between. I (sort of) had a boyfriend and went to prom, but even that relationship never moved beyond hand holding and the occasional kiss hello or good-bye. I told myself it was because I was a "good girl," but the reality was that I couldn't jump the hurdles required for an in-depth, intimate relationship. SPD and general dysfunction kept me locked inside myself, unable to set foot outside my extremely tiny comfort zone.

INTIMACY CAN BE WONDERFUL, FROM WHAT I CAN DEDUCE
MARLENE GOMEZ

Don't even get me talking about dating. How hard it is to try to date when the lightest touch makes you feel like vomiting and hitting the person next to you! How difficult to flirt if you can't make eye contact!

My first kiss was awful. The guy didn't know it was my first and French-kissed me. I found it revolting and had a very honest reaction, saying something like: "Yuck!" Being hyperreactive made every step of the way in dating become a difficult road to travel.

But intimacy can be wonderful later, since sensory overresponsivity sort of makes it more intense, from what I can deduce talking to other people. A good make-out session with a wonderful partner can become the best regulator ever.

KISSES, NO; HUGS, YES
JUDY MCCARTER

Navigating dating rituals is difficult enough for "neurotypicals" (whatever neurotypical is). For those of us with SPD, it can be especially unpleasant. Getting ready for a date was torture because "pretty" meant wearing tight, scratchy clothing. I wore a jacket to limit skin contact from the guy's arm creeping around my shoulders at the movies.

And, oh, those pantyhose! They made me feel itchy, like I had bugs crawling up my legs.

I was put off if boys were physically assertive. Hand holding and friendly touching made me very uncomfortable.

I have always been verbally social. Conversation was more about participating in the dating process than being truly interested in the fellows. Often, they mistook my conversation as a sign of devotion, when I was trying to distract them and keep their hands off me!

At one point, I thought talking in a parked car was better than in public areas, where nearby conversations drove me crazy. However, I found that smaller spaces meant closer proximity and more touching without options for a quick escape. Using the restroom or getting an upset stomach was a way to avoid closeness.

Eating out, I preferred a quiet booth to decrease auditory input and put space between me and my date. Booth benches across from each other mean you can have a physical boundary and still be socially appropriate.

Eating was nerve-racking because I was so clumsy. I would end up with food on my clothing, face, or hands or knock a glass over and silverware off the table. The food always gave me indigestion, so I would go through the date trying not to burp. Back then, the guy always paid for the meal, so I felt obligated to eat it.

Going to movies was awful. The scent of aftershave and perfume made me get severe migraines and then throw up. The sound in theaters was so intense that I would escape to the restroom. Most of my dates probably thought I had bladder control issues.

I was no fun at amusement parks. I refused to go on rides because I would get dizzy and throw up. Heights also made me sick and extremely fearful.

My clumsiness showed at the bowling alley. I was the "Gutter Ball Queen." I was also weird about using a bowling ball because the temperature was colder inside the finger holes than outside. Bowling shoes were torture. They were too tight, and my feet felt suffocated, not to mention the nauseating smell. My proprioception is off, and I couldn't tell how much force I put behind the ball. I felt I wasn't using enough force but actually used too much, and my dates would say, "You're going to break the floor."

Trying to keep score is hard with visual perceptual problems. My scorekeeping was always inaccurate, so I'd "play dumb." After several attempts to teach me, my dates would become irritated. Little did they know I felt I was learning something new every time and that I'd never be able to learn the procedures because of the stressful environment.

Then, the kissing part that guys seemed to like always made me uncomfortable. I wanted to get it over with because I could taste their breath mints. I did, however, love tight, long good night hugs.

For adolescents with SPD, already overloaded with uncomfortable clothes, overstimulating environments, baffling activities, and perhaps distasteful meals, kissing may be the last straw. They may bolt from kisses but beg for hugs. For kissing to be fun, or even feasible, conditions must be just right. Ideally, the kisser is understanding and someone the kissee trusts and wants to snuggle up to. The kisser gives notice that a kiss is coming up and doesn't pounce. The kisser prepares the kissee with a long, strong, calming bear hug. The kissee feels safe, not trapped.

Maybe that's a lot to ask for.

Consider how conditions were far from just right for Meredith Joseph Blaine when he and a sensory craver met head-on.

MY DATE WITH "M"
MEREDITH JOSEPH BLAINE

I was about twenty, long before I knew I had SPD or ASD, when my employer set me up for a first date with a coworker, "M."

It first seemed harmless enough as M and I, together with her family, were watching a basketball game. After the game, she and I sat alone on the sofa. We were talking, and she started to become more intimate. She got ever closer and truly invaded my comfort zone. She started to kiss me on the lips, and my body and mind became confused by her completely unexpected eroticism, coupled with my high degree of tactile defensiveness.

She told me to "just relax," and I was about halfway out of my skin. She kissed me again on the lips while moving more of her body my way. I am sure that it was sudden eroticism for her, while I was most uncomfortable with my body and senses being very overloaded! I moved away and tried to regain my composure in every sense of the word, while at the same time trying not to hurt her feelings.

Fortunately for us, the evening ended on much calmer terms. She, in fact, drove me back home a short time later.

I think that M was infatuated with me, and I do not think that she was all there, in many respects. She was immature and may have had issues with social skills, too. After all, I do not believe that kissing on the lips is the way to begin a first date. And, of course, someone like myself with social skills issues, too, did not make for a first successful boyfriend/girlfriend relationship.

Universally, everyone's first romantic encounters are emotion packed and inelegant, rarely meeting anybody's great expectations. Kissing and petting may make young people uncomfortable or even frightened.

Usually, it does get better. How? With praxis, praxis, praxis! (See the following box.)

THE FIRST KISS AND PRAXIS

A romantic kiss requires abilities that take time for teenagers to develop—social skills, verbal communication, motor coordination, self-control, planning, sequencing, and conscious thought. In other words, a kiss requires praxis.

Praxis is the typical, everyday, desirable end result of efficient sensory processing (see chapter 2, "Primer" page 17 to review *praxis* and page 38 to review *dyspraxia*, a subtype of SPD). For many people with SPD, having good praxis takes time, patience, and many rehearsals. Once you have good praxis, you may interact successfully with people and the physical environment and do what you need and want to do. Good praxis has three components:

Ideation—A person conceives of an idea to do something. For example, Boy comes up with the idea of kissing Girl.

Planning—Boy plans the Kiss in a rudimentary fashion, as he doesn't know what he's doing and can't think of everything. The Kiss will involve an organized sequence of several complex, unfamiliar actions that employ most senses. If all senses are in sync, the Kiss will go more smoothly.

Execution—Boy carries out his plan. Thought, action, and sensory processing come together, as he:

- Sits down (vestibular, proprioceptive) with Girl on a bench,
- Turns toward her (vestibular) and gazes into her eyes (visual),
- Tells her he really likes her and hears her tell him the same (auditory),
- Slowly leans forward (vestibular, proprioceptive),
- Strokes her hair (tactile),
- Puts his hands confidently around her shoulders and

> draws her close with the just-right force (tactile, pro-
> prioceptive),
> • Inhales her sweet scent (olfactory), and
> • Kisses her lips (tactile, gustatory, and, by this time,
> probably interoceptive, too).
>
> The more practice you have with this—or any—complex
> activity, the more inner drive you will have to ideate, plan,
> and execute further pleasant experiences.

If the first hand holding, the first kiss, the first skin-to-skin contact, or the "first time" go well, that is a gift but not a given for anybody, particularly for teenagers with SPD. Difficulties with touching, communicating, timing, being cool, and so forth may get in their way. Disheartened, they may come to believe that romance is too complicated, embarrassing, and awkward, and they are simply no good at it.

The good news is that these initial disappointments can change with maturity, experience, and the right partners. The sensation of being overstimulated may add to the excitement in a pleasing way. Also, the compression of bear hugs and the deep pressure of sexual activity may be therapeutically calming, making intimacy desirable, satisfying, and joyful, according to nature's plan.

SEX AS A THERAPY TOOL
SHONDA LUCAS

My first experiences were quite unsexy—not exactly what you'd call romantic or like Hollywood makes us believe they're supposed to be.

My very low self-esteem enhanced that first-time awkwardness to an extreme. I was anxious about my role—what if I didn't like how things felt, or what if my senses got overloaded and I freaked out a little, or worse? Plus, when I get overstimulated, I lose coordination, which made undressing more like a circus act than something sensual. I recall fumbling with fasteners and buttons and feeling like a complete idiot.

To me, the act of sex is a whole-body experience—touch, smell, taste, sound, sight, movement, etc. Like dance, there is a certain rhythm to it. Where else am I going to use all of my senses at once?

In some ways sex is comparable to occupational therapy techniques. Sometimes I crave the heaviness of deep pressure, and I admit I've used sex as a therapy tool to help deal with overstimulation in my everyday world.

Luckily, as I matured, I learned to use that overstimulated feeling to my advantage during the act itself. Sex quickly replaced my desire to wrestle or roughhouse with my guy friends. I also learned how to control my anxieties (and how to unfasten my bra gracefully), making intimate relationships much less awkward and eventually something that I enjoy.

Maintaining romantic relationships takes a lot of work. When one partner has SPD and the other is typical, what is their relationship like? It is like any arrangement in which two people make accommodations for each other. To cope with sensory challenges and function well, the task is to balance independence whenever possible with the just-right support whenever necessary.

Just as important as getting support is participating in life together. Here, a teenager writes to her imaginary partner who, she hopes, will wholly understand her as well as wholeheartedly join in her experiences.

TO MY FUTURE HUSBAND
OR EVEN FUTURE VERY BEST FRIEND
(IF I LET YOU IN)
LECIA BAKER

You will see me pressing my body into a wall.

I will lie on the floor and roll back and forth.

You will see me ride a bike,

Click my pen and tap on things.

You will see me swing on a swing,

Bounce on an exercise ball,

Do wall push-ups.

You will see earplugs and headphones and bracelets.

I'm sorry, but I will seek out every sensation from material things
    before I even contemplate a hug.

I will bite my lip and scratch myself when things go wrong . . .

Or guess what? . . . when there's no place to lean against so each
    part of my skin feels something!

I cannot leave my skin floating in air!

I will secretly do things that other people don't pay attention to that
    get rid of the icky feelings,

And I hope you never see me cut.

You will see me roll on the floor in anger because sometimes even
    deep pressure doesn't feel right.

You will see me cry.

You will see me shake my leg

And open all your doors for you.

Most importantly, when you see me swing, bounce, spin, or rock
    with my eyes closed—

Meaning that my whole body shouts with fantastic feelings that en-
    gulf my body and make me smile and giggle for a moment be-

cause there's something about it that just feels perfect, and
   this world will never understand—
You will know that I trust you with every bit of myself
Because I trust that you love me for me,
And you will know that I have welcomed you into my world.
I hope one day instead of just seeing
You will know, without a word, that exactly what I need is a hug from
   behind,
Or for you to rock with me
Swing with me
Laugh with me
Do wall push-ups with me
Take away the knife
And give me a super-tight squeeze (even when I deny),
Stomp with me, spin with me
Lie on the ground with me
Look me in the eye and say everything is all right.
Thanks for entering my world.
I wish you would never leave.

When finding that special, understanding person—and letting that
person in—occurs, this is no surprise to me; I think people with
SPD are very lovable. Being typical is not a requirement for loving
and being loved. When both partners learn to see and know each
other, and when the sensory environment is just right, a mutually
satisfying relationship can evolve.

THE AFFECTION THING
MELISSA PALMER

Of all the things I've adjusted to while being with my husband, Bob, his style of affection has been the hardest. His fear of crowds? No problem; we can have fun without concerts and malls. His aversion to crunchy vegetables? I put them on the side. That kind of adjustment was a piece of cake, compared to the affection thing.

Imagine dating someone who never kissed you. Imagine reaching for a suitor's hand that he snaps out of your grasp, or trying to lean your head on someone's shoulder only to have him lean away. That's how it was with Bob.

He doesn't like touching. Period. In every situation.

If you hug him, his whole body goes rigid, and he pulls away as your arms close around him. You could be his kid, his mom, his spouse. You could be handing him the Publishers Clearing House check for a million dollars, but if you try to hug him while you do it, he'll go cold. If you sit close to him on the couch, he will scoot over until he's balancing on the armrest to get away.

With hand holding, Bob finds it difficult to gauge how hard he's squeezing. Most of the time, the answer is, very. If I do get him to twine his fingers in mine, I grit my teeth while his grip grinds my bones. Meanwhile, his body stiffens, and his face looks like he's hoping not to get stung by a menacing bee.

All that preamble stuff that goes along with physical romance is lost on both of us, because for him none of it is pleasant. Nonetheless, he has the same biological impulse that every red-blooded man gets usually right before the moon is full. For both of us, lovemaking doesn't need a long warm-up to feel like fireworks!

Recently, after being together for years, he opened up to me and said that when someone hugs him, it feels physically uncomfortable. Nothing about it feels right. Then comes a feeling of anxiety he can't make sense of, just like he gets in a big crowd, like at any moment something awful is about to happen.

Until he told me about his physical discomfort, I don't think I could truly understand what he goes through on a daily basis. I felt selfish and ashamed for all the years I spent wishing he could hug me or sweep me up in his arms like in the romance stories. All those feelings were replaced by the overwhelming need to show him that I understand.

I can't count on a kiss in the morning. I might not get a comforting hug during an emotional time. Yet, I am more than satisfied with my thoughtful, caring husband and the fireworks we share.

For Bob, and now for me, physical affection does not equal love, which is not the typical view in marriage. But I married Bob for the same reason I love him—he is not typical at all.

LIFE AFTER DATING
JUDY MCCARTER

The good news is that there is life after dating, and it is called predictable, consistent, boring marriage. And, guess what? You don't have to wear pantyhose!

Finding someone you love and wanting to be with that person will motivate you to deal with some of your irritants and help you tolerate them. Also, your husband will grow to understand you and no longer wear aftershave if the smells bother you, won't suggest eating at the midnight taco place or expect you to always wear makeup, and will let you have your own space on the couch. He won't care if you love living in pajamas and watching movies at home instead of going out. What your spouse will get in return is gratitude for allowing you to be your authentic and unique, eccentric self.

Freedom to be an atypical, authentic, and unique individual is what adolescents with SPD hope and strive for. Empowered with that freedom, they may love and be loved as well as anyone in the world.

COPING TIPS FOR COMMON DATING CHALLENGES

IF YOU DO NOT KNOW THE PERSON WELL:

- Agree to a short date. Perhaps you could take a walk. If the person turns out to be not to your liking, at least you get some exercise!
- Decide how much information to reveal about your SPD. You may decide to tell your partner right away, or to refer to symptoms without getting deeply into an explanation of the disorder. Remember that spilling the beans too much, too soon, about your particular challenges could make a date feel uncomfortable or nervous.

IF YOU ARE UNCOMFORTABLE BEING TOUCHED, HELD, OR KISSED:

- Realize that a certain percentage of the discomfort will be anxiety. At the right time you may be able to experience pleasure from being close.
- Before setting out on the date, do some self-therapy. Take a hot shower, massage some lotion into your arms and hands, or do some form of exercise—whatever you have found helps you organize your nervous system.
- Before and during the date, use deep-breathing strategies. You can breathe deeply while sitting in a movie, reading a menu, or visiting the restroom.

- If your date's reaching for you is too much, tell him that you like him, but that you are just one of those people who needs a bit of space when you're getting to know someone.
- Use body language to communicate your needs. If she hugs you, give her a quick squeeze back and then release her. She will likely back off. Don't walk too close if you would like him not to put his arm around you.
- If kissing is uncomfortable or "too wet," remind yourself that this is a very new experience. Don't panic. It can begin to feel nice, once you feel more comfortable on the date. If you'd like only a dry kiss, use body language to communicate that by keeping your lips shut. When you are ready for a deeper kiss, you'll know what to do.

IF THE SENSORY ENVIRONMENT OF THE DATE MAKES YOU UNCOMFORTABLE:

- Before going out on the date, find out where you will be going. That way you can either possibly make a change or at least make some sort of plan that will allow you to leave early if you become overwhelmed. But before you bolt, try to give yourself a little practice hanging in with the discomfort. Next time it happens, you may be more comfortable.
- If it is too noisy, after a little while tell him you can't really hear him talk, and ask if you could go someplace more quiet. Explain you have always been really sensitive to loud noises.
- If the lights are too bright and flashing, tell your date you tend to get headaches with so much crazy lighting, and would she mind if you don't stay too long.

TO MAINTAIN A LOVING RELATIONSHIP:

- Explain to your partner what sensations cause you to panic, get angry, shut down, or otherwise flip out. With knowledge, he or she can help you get you out of an uncomfortable situation and calm down.
- When your partner prefers to sit back and watch movies but you need invigorating, sensory-rich hikes (or vice versa), take turns doing what the other person loves to do. Reciprocity is the name of the game.
- Remember that love and respect, not dependence and pity, are the glue that hold your relationship together.
- Give each other at least twelve hugs a day—especially if your partner enjoys deep pressure!
- Laugh together.

PART IV

LIVING AN "IN-SYNC" LIFE

CHAPTER 12

Treating SPD

So far, we have heard how ordinary experiences present extraordinary challenges to teenagers growing up with SPD. People who don't live with SPD may have no idea that daily activities and human relationships can be so complicated and formidable.

Is it possible to live successfully with SPD?

Many people living with SPD say yes, and each in a different way.

Each person's path toward a successful life is unique and involves a combination of self-awareness, maturation, family support, do-it-yourself treatments, and, for many, professional therapy and guidance.

- Self-awareness—As young people grow to recognize their SPD, they learn to anticipate potentially stressful sensory experiences and discover compensatory strategies. Thus, for the sake of self-preservation, they stay away from noisy pep rallies, or they go regularly to the gym for peppy workouts. They avoid spicy food, or they crave spicy food. They do what it takes to feel safe and to cope.
- Maturation—Some sensory processing difficulties may

207

decrease or become only a vague memory as children grow into adolescence.

- Family support—The sooner adolescents (and their families) understand the reason for their symptoms, the sooner they can begin to explore treatment options.

- Do-it-yourself treatments—Many adolescents with SPD come up with techniques that cost little or nothing and bring relief.

- Professional therapy—The wisest and most common treatment is occupational therapy using a sensory integrative approach, or OT-SI.

- Implementing Dr. Lucy Jane Miller's problem-solving method, called A SECRET.

Described below are occupational therapy using a sensory integration approach, other appropriate therapies for SPD, and Dr. Miller's method of problem solving.

OCCUPATIONAL THERAPY (OT-SI)

Occupational therapy (OT) is a broad-ranging health profession that includes direct treatment, home programs, education, and/or accommodations for people of all ages, from infants to centenarians. Although young children with more malleable (neuroplastic) brains improve faster, adults and adolescents also benefit from intervention. The human brain is continually developing, changing, and making adaptations, even into old age.

Occupational therapy using a sensory integration approach (OT-SI) is designed to improve sensory processing and decrease atypical reactions to ordinary sensations. The occupational therapist (also abbreviated "OT") who specializes in sensory processing issues uses specific tactile stimulation, movement, balancing, sounds, and other sensory experiences to reduce the client's over-reactivity to sensory input. Adolescents and young adults who have been uncomfortable with sensory experiences involving touch, movement, or heights can change and become much more success-ful and happy during those activities.

OTs are in a position to educate adolescents about their sen-sory systems to help them understand how their particular sensory processing difficulties affect learning, relationships, and social par-ticipation. This understanding lays the foundation for developing smart strategies to reduce SPD's negative impact on their daily life.

OT-SI addresses everyday life skills, such as:

- Tactile responsivity and discrimination
- Balance and postural control
- Body awareness and gravitational security
- Ideation, planning, and execution of complex, volun-tary actions (praxis)
- Gross motor coordination
- Flexion and extension
- Fine motor coordination
- Bilateral integration and coordination
- Eye-motor (ocular-motor or visual-motor) skills
- Visual perception and discrimination
- Self-help
- Self-esteem
- Social participation
- Organization, using a paper or electronic planner

With or without regular direct treatment, sensory programs for home and school, planned by the OT with input from the client, family members, and teachers, are also useful. Involvement from family and perhaps friends, too, can make the program not only beneficial but also fun and emotionally satisfying.

Someone at school may be able to suggest an OT who practices sensory integration techniques and also works with teenagers. (OTs who concentrate on improving handwriting and fine motor tasks, who are not trained in SI techniques, and who work best with young children may be wonderful people but less helpful.) If an OT's evaluation shows that your teenager's challenges at school warrant "related services," the school is obligated to provide them for free.

Finding an Occupational Therapist

Hiring an OT privately may work for your family, especially if your insurance plan provides coverage. Here are some suggestions for finding an OT:

- Ask your pediatrician, family doctor, local health center, or parent advocacy organization for a referral.
- Check out https://findanoccupationaltherapist.com. In Canada, go to www.caot.ca/index.asp.
- Search the Internet for an SPD support group. A member may be able to suggest an appropriate OT near you.
- The American Occupational Therapy Association (www.aota.org) may be helpful.
- Locate a therapist at the STAR Institute's National SPD Treatment Directory at www.spdstar.org. This is a one-of-a-kind guide to services. The list includes more than 2,500 health care, education, and community service providers who have experience and expertise in working with adolescents with SPD and

other special needs. (Note that a listing does not constitute an endorsement by the STAR Institute, and no guarantee is implied that the providers' information is accurate or up-to-date.) Providers include:

- Occupational therapists
- Physical therapists
- Speech-and-language pathologists
- Mental health professionals
- Physicians
- Optometrists and other eye care specialists
- Dentists
- Educators and school counselors
- Community resources, such as libraries, recreation centers, and hair salons

If you can get to Colorado, seek out intensive sessions from STAR Institute (Sensory Therapies and Research), founded by Dr. Lucy Jane Miller. The center has recently begun offering an adolescent/adult program that gives OT and mental health support on a daily basis for short-term clients. Get assessed and get daily consultation for as many days as you can afford. Back home, you can continue getting support via Skype or Zoom. Your time and money will be well spent.

SPD Scientific Work Group

Growing evidence shows the efficacy of OT-SI. Exciting research is being conducted by the SPD Scientific Work Group (SPD-SWG) in an initiative funded by the Wallace Research Foundation. Dr. Lucy Jane Miller has been assigned with the task of finding and vetting scientists interested in studying SPD. Each year, five or six scientists receive funding for their work. The renowned scientists on the SPD-

SWG represent multiple disciplines and come together regularly to discuss their findings about many questions, including:

- What are the causes of SPD?
- Is SPD a disorder that exists without other disorders, or is it only a comorbid (co-occurring) symptom of autism spectrum disorder (ASD), ADHD, OCD, etc.?
- What is the prevalence of SPD separately and as a co-occurring condition?
- What are the observable characteristics and risk factors? How early can they be reliably identified?
- What is the neurophysiological basis of SPD?
- What are treatments for SPD? Which work effectively?
- How does SPD affect the family?
- What is the developmental trajectory of SPD?

Among the OTs in the scientific work group who have done important studies on SPD in adolescents and young adults are Moya Kinnealey, PhD, Teresa May-Benson, ScD, Lucy Jane Miller, PhD, Sarah A. Schoen, PhD, and the late Jane Koomar, PhD. Learn more at www.spdstar.org.

OTHER THERAPIES FOR ADOLESCENTS WITH SPD

Especially when provided in conjunction with occupational therapy using a sensory integration approach (OT-SI), other therapies may also be appropriate. Of course, too much therapy can be counterproductive if it limits the teenager's time for more socially and emotionally satisfying activities. No one should have all these therapies at the same time. Consider trying a therapy when the adolescent is having a particularly hard time in a specific area of his life.

For instance, if he is having difficulty articulating his words and communicating his needs and thoughts, look into speech-and-language therapy. If she complains of tired eyes and has a hard time with reading assignments, see a behavioral optometrist.

- Physical therapy (PT) is a health profession addressing neuromuscular and orthopedic conditions such as poor motor planning and coordination, low muscle tone, and decreased strength, stability, and stamina. PT may improve a person's motor control and physical coordination, especially of the large muscles. A physical therapist (also abbreviated "PT") may use massage, whirlpool baths, or ultrasound to help clients get their muscles ready for voluntary movement. The adolescent or young adult with SPD will be best served by a PT who has received additional training in sensory integration theory and treatment (PT-SI). (See www.apta.org or www.spdstar.org.)

- Vision therapy (VT), akin to PT and OT, is specifically for the eyes and brain. A doctor of optometry, called a behavioral optometrist or developmental optometrist, addresses vision problems, including lazy eye, crossed eyes, double vision, and convergence insufficiency. The optometrist may help the person integrate visual information with input from other senses, such as hearing, touching, and moving. Vision therapy may include eyeglasses with traditional or specialized lenses (prisms), in addition to sensory-motor and educational activities that strengthen the person's ocular-motor control, visual discrimination, and eye-hand coordination. While VT helps to resolve some reading and learning problems, behavioral optometrists are quick to disclaim that the therapy *directly* treats learning disabilities. (See www.optometrists.org, www.covd.org, or www.spdstar.org.)

• Listening therapy (LT) may help people integrate sensory input by using specific sound frequencies and patterns to stimulate the brain. LT is based on the theory of neuroplasticity, referring to brain changes that occur as a result of specific, repeated stimulation. OTs, as well as professionals in many other fields, may become certified to provide LT. Several widely used programs include auditory integration therapy (AIT), Therapeutic Listening (from Vital Links), Samonas sound therapy, and the Listening Program. Some programs include music specifically arranged for sleeping. The most scientifically validated listening therapy is Integrated Listening Systems (iLs), a multisensory program. It starts with movement and music (delivered via iPod in a portable waist pack) and gradually integrates language and cognitive processes. The three main systems for organizing sensory input—visual, auditory, and vestibular—are highly interrelated. Stimulating all three at the same time is a holistic approach that may help people of all ages and developmental stages to feel more focused and self-confident. (See www.integratedlistening.com or www.spdstar .org.)

• Psychotherapy, provided by a psychotherapist, clinical psychologist, or licensed clinical social worker, may be helpful if the teenager or young adult has behavior or self-image problems or is depressed or anxious, owing to years of poor sensory processing. (Psychotherapy deals with the secondary, emotional effects of SPD but not with the underlying causes.) Types of psychotherapy include cognitive behavioral therapy (CBT), to help a person address irrational or distorted thoughts, feelings, and behaviors, and family therapy, to help the adolescent, parents, and siblings become a healthier unit. A form of CBT is the metacognitive approach ("thinking about thinking") in which a person uses specific strategies for learning or problem solving. (See www.spdstar.org.)

- Speech-and-language pathology (SLP) may help the adolescent strengthen expressive and/or receptive communication. Specific goals may be improving speech skills, such as pronouncing *l*, *k*, or *sh* sounds; monitoring the pitch of the person's voice; and strengthening mouth muscles for oral-motor control. Activities to expand language skills include conversing and developing memory and vocabulary. A speech pathologist trained in oral-motor and feeding issues may also be able to help the selective eater. (See www.asha.org or www.spdstar.org.)

- Several young people with SPD report having benefited from these therapies and alternative approaches, which may also incorporate SI techniques:

  - Deep pressure and proprioceptive technique (known as brushing), for helping reduce tactile overresponsivity
  - Nutritional therapy, identifying and addressing difficulties with health, diet, eating, and daily functioning
  - Perceptual-motor therapy, providing integrated movement experiences that remediate gross motor, fine motor, and visual perception problems
  - Hatha yoga, involving physical exercises (known as asanas or postures), designed to align muscles and bones and to increase energy and well-being
  - Massage, providing deep pressure and tactile input that may be both physically and emotionally soothing while increasing body awareness

- Martial arts, using physical skill and motor coordination without weapons, such as karate, aikido, judo, or kung fu
- Craniosacral therapy, using light touch manipulation of the bones in the skull, sacrum, and coccyx to improve sensory, motor, and neurological function

- Not only physical therapists, optometrists, clinical psychologists, and speech-and-language pathologists, but also some school counselors, pediatricians, and other specialists working with children and adolescents incorporate SI techniques into their practice. Several of my favorite books about collaboration among therapists include *No Longer A SECRET: Unique Common Sense Strategies for Children with Sensory or Motor Challenges* by Doreit S. Bialer and Lucy Jane Miller, (2011); *The Sensory Connection: An OT and SLP Team Approach* by Nancy Kashman and Janet Mora (2005); *Sensory Processing Challenges: Effective Clinical Work with Kids and Teens* by Lindsey Biel (2014); and *Outsmarting Autism: The Ultimate Guide to Management, Healing, and Prevention* by Patricia S. Lemer (2014).

Foremost among the above list of helpful books and techniques is *No Longer A SECRET*. It outlines an excellent way for parents and teachers to help their young people with SPD and merits a discussion here.

PROBLEM SOLVING USING DR. LUCY JANE MILLER'S METHOD: A SECRET

Adolescents and young adults with SPD frequently feel uncomfortable or get "stuck" in sensory situations. One way to improve these situations is to get familiar with a problem-solving method that OTs and other therapists call "clinical reasoning." This involves analyzing what's happening inside and outside the teenager and then thinking of modifications.

At STAR Institute in Colorado, Lucy Jane Miller, PhD, OTR, has developed a problem-solving method called A SECRET. She lays it out in her books *Sensational Kids* (revised, 2014) and, coauthored by Doreit Bialer, *No Longer A SECRET* (2011).

Lucy teaches parents, teenagers, and even young children to analyze seven elements in sensory or motor challenges and to suggest ideas that may lead to smoother functioning. This is a preventive approach.

"A SECRET" is an acronym for these seven elements: attention, sensation, emotional regulation, culture (including context and current conditions), relationship, environment, and task. A SECRET is not a rigid formula for *what to do*, but a flexible format for *how to think* about manipulating these elements.

First you choose one challenging area, such as self-help skills. Then there are questions a parent (or whoever is involved) can ponder when a teenager is struggling with, say, the sensory-motor problem of getting dressed. Here is an example.

A = Can I do something to change my son's *attention* to his problem? I could suggest that he search online for organic, fair trade clothes that appeal to his interests, or for soft, seamless items that meet his sensory specifications, to help him attend to what he wears.

S = Can I find a great *sensory* strategy? A morning back rub or rolling a therapy ball over him may get input into his skin and muscles to ready him to get dressed.

E = Can he do something to affect his *emotional* regulation in the moment? Perhaps playing his favorite upbeat music or brightening (or dimming) the lighting in his room would get him in the mood to get dressed.

C = What could I change about the *culture/context/current* conditions? (This doesn't refer to ethnic culture; it specifically focuses on how things are done at home or wherever the challenge occurs.) Dressing after breakfast, rather than before, may make a difference, or doing a clothes-oriented chore like washing or putting away his own clothes.

R = Is there something about our *relationship* that I could use to motivate his dressing? Letting him wear what's comfortable, and not telling him what looks best, may help him get dressed quickly. It may work to take him shopping on a quiet weeknight and allow him to select new clothes.

E = What in our *environment* could I change? It may help to install hooks in his closet so he needn't fuss with hangers, or to set up labeled bins ("T-shirts," "Socks," etc.), instead of a visually confusing jumble in a dresser drawer. A dressing schedule posted on the wall may be useful, too.

T = Can I add or subtract a *task* to change the situation? He could lay out his clothes the night before, or use a visual schedule and check off each item when he puts it on.

Implementing A SECRET takes a bit of practice, as do all worthwhile and life-changing endeavors. It can not only have a major impact on the teenager but also make school and family life much smoother. For example, you could take this idea to an Individualized Education Program (IEP) meeting and involve all the teachers in the problem-solving tasks. Or you could take it to Grandma's before Thanksgiving dinner and get the family involved in ways to make the big gathering work for your teenager.

SENSORY LIFESTYLE

Putting together all the pieces can lead to a sensory lifestyle. This is an individual's way of living that incorporates—or eliminates—sensory stimuli to help the person function smoothly in daily life. For people with SPD, a sensory lifestyle includes sensory integration techniques that an occupational therapist develops to help the person become more self-regulated, alert, and engaged.

And for *everyone*, like you and me, with or without SPD, a sensory lifestyle includes:

- Avoiding sensory triggers that cause pain or discomfort
- Seeking out multisensory experiences that are satisfying and restore order
- Eating a healthful diet with crunchy vegetables, whole grains, protein, etc.
- Avoiding sugar, soda, beer, cigarettes, marijuana, and other harmful substances
- Sleeping eight and a half to nine and a half hours each night

• Doing heavy work activity that involves pushing, pull-
    ing, lifting, and carrying, such as vacuuming, mow-
    ing, lifting weights, and carrying books and laundry
• Spending time outdoors every day, such as walking to
    school or work
• Spending time relating to other people at school, work,
    meals, and out and about

TREATMENT STORIES

Now let's look at how young people with SPD feel about their experiences with occupational therapy. Other stories describe orthodontia and do-it-yourself treatments that have worked well for
them.

Before writing her piece, Leanna Taylor needed a refresher
about her childhood sensory difficulties, because her memories of
OT-SI were dim. She unearthed an assessment written by an occupational therapist who had evaluated Leanna's neurological development when she was six. Leanna uses the OT's statements as a
scaffold for her piece about growing up with unique "sensory tics."
Reading Leanna's words, you will see how far the out-of-sync six-
year-old—with tactile, visual, and vestibular dysfunction—has
come. Today she is a typical teenager who, just like everybody
else, has more than one side to her personality, preferences, and
identity.

EVERYONE HAS MORE THAN ONE SIDE
LEANNA TAYLOR

(Note: The occupational therapist's comments when Leanna was six are in this font.

Leanna's comments, written ten years later, are in this font.)

Occupational Therapist (OT): Leanna is a 6.4-year-old girl who was referred for evaluation by her parents and pediatrician. Major concerns expressed by Mrs. Taylor are toe walking, clumsiness, sensory defensive behaviors, car sickness, and emotional outbursts. She also has language problems relating to semantics.

Leanna: And now, Leanna is a 16.6-year-old girl whose major concerns are AP classes, getting her learner's permit, and figuring out how she'll get thirteen dollars for hair dye. I sound like a normal teenager, right? Well, of course, I am, but that's only one side of me.

When you're a teenager like me, it's hard to explain what SPD is, specifically to another teenager, because besides your family, the people that you want to understand you the most are your friends. The only thing I could tell them was that I can't take in too many sensations at once, that I have what I like to call "sensory tics" that can overwhelm me sometimes, and that SPD is unique to each person. Then they'd ask me how it's unique to me, and that's where I usually got lost. I didn't know how to explain my sensory tics because I didn't know what all of them were. So my mom gave me my occupational therapy evaluation from when I was six.

OT: Her mother reports that Leanna is easily frustrated and will often cut things (hair, paper, etc.) into small pieces when angry.

Leanna: I don't remember cutting things up when I was six. Then again, I don't remember most things from when I was little. The fact that I've grown out of this defense mechanism is good. Nobody wants to be around an angry teenager with scissors. I giggled a little as I reread the sentence, because all I could think about was how troublesome I must have been. Now I've taken a calmer route to deal with my anger; listening to heavy metal music definitely has its benefits.

OT: She W-sits[1] when not in a chair and does not respond well to being corrected.

Leanna: Would it be surprising that I am sitting in that same position as I read the report? Even after therapeutic intervention, I still W-sit. It's comfortable!

OT: Fine motor skills are within normal limits. She has excellent cursive handwriting for her age.[2]

Leanna: I've always been proud of my handwriting skills. My friends have pointed out that my cursive is "like, so, so, so much better" than theirs! I've been told that I should make my own font for word processing, which actually sounds pretty cool.

---

1   To "W-sit" is to sit with buttocks on the floor and legs folded, knees forward and on the floor and feet out to the sides. For people with low muscle tone and poor balance, W-sitting provides wider stability than sitting with legs crossed in an X. Sitting against a wall or in a seat with a supportive back helps.

2   The therapist praises Leanna's excellent handwriting, one of her strengths. Frequently, inefficient tactile and proprioceptive processing interferes with holding and writing with a pencil. With determination and practice, however, a person can develop remarkable handwriting. This is a "splinter skill," which is an isolated, unexpected, high-level ability in a person with challenges.

OT: Leanna walks and runs on her toes.[3] She is able to do a proper heel strike with verbal cues to "put your heels down, take larger steps, and slow down." Her left heel cord is slightly tight, which encourages toe walking.

Leanna: Toe walking is one thing I remember from my childhood. I have no idea why I did that. My mom says it had to do with my sense of balance, which wasn't so good. I used to tell myself that I toe walked because I had a secret desire to be the world's greatest ballerina. I did take ballet, but I grew out of that; it's too girly for me.

OT: She frequently bumps into things, trips, and falls.

Leanna: When I first read this, I thought, "Okay, this therapist lady is being ridiculous. Everyone can be klutzy. She probably just wanted to fill in some random crap to fill in all the spaces on a long list." But then I started to piece things together. I thought about all the times I ran into things because I thought they were further away than they actually were. I remember all the times I miscounted the steps and ended up tripping or falling. My body was always decorated with bruises from constantly bumping into the furniture, doors, railings, and kitchen counters. (And don't ask me how I could injure myself with a kitchen counter. It just happens!) I sighed and realized that she was right: I lacked spatial awareness.

---

3 Toe walking may be caused by vestibular, proprioceptive, tactile, or visual dysfunction. Bumping into things, inability to ride a bike, and dizziness could also be vestibular or visual issues. An OT or a developmental optometrist may be able to diagnose what is causing sensory difficulties like these.

OT: She is unable to ride a two-wheel bicycle.

Leanna: Even now, the closest I can get to riding a bike is our workout bike, which is planted firmly to the ground, not relying on me to keep it up straight, just the way I like it. Once again, this is due to my shaky sense of balance. I'm not going to bother trying to learn how to ride. I enjoy long walks, and, besides, there's always the public bus for the colder days.

OT: She becomes dizzy easily and has severe car sickness, indicating vestibular deficit.

Leanna: Oh, fancy medical terms, how I adore you! I had to google that term and learned "vestibular deficit" basically means that my body's balance system was dysfunctional, and I could get overly dizzy to the point where I threw up. The OT could have just said, "Your daughter has a lot of problems with balance." Luckily, this was one of the sensory tics that went away over the years, so now I can enjoy long car rides and ride the roller coasters at Six Flags amusement park (but nothing with a huge drop).

OT: Leanna exhibits moderate to severe sensory defensive behaviors.

Leanna: I couldn't exactly wrap my head around "sensory defensive behaviors." So I went to my mom for a blunt translation, and she told me that I used to exhibit behaviors that showed that I didn't like being touched, such as pulling away from someone who would put a hand on my shoulder. And even though I said "used to," that doesn't mean I don't hate it anymore; but that also doesn't mean I still hate it.

Don't get me wrong, I love hugs. I need at least one hug a day so that I feel like my day is complete, but everyone gets hugged out at some point. Sometimes I can't stand it when friends are being too touchy with me. It will get to the point where I want to shake them off and make them stand where they can't reach me. I've tried explaining it before, but unfortunately, some people just don't get it.

While the report was helpful, I knew that there was so much left out. It probably covered only half of my sensory tics. When some went away as I grew up, others came. I could probably go on for days about other little things that make chills run laps up and down my spine and give me piercing headaches.

When I tell people that I have SPD, they're usually confused and shocked, because I seem so normal in their eyes. Some would ask if I "grew out of it." I learned to control it. SPD is now one of my many quirks that lie hidden in the deepest layer within me.

Everyone has more than one side. On one side, I'm still Leanna the dysfunctional six-year-old who W-sits, walks on her toes, and cuts things when frustrated. On the other side, I'm Leanna the sixteen-year-old who keeps the six-year-old securely on her feet and makes sure she's out of reach from the scissors.

You see, it *can* get better. A little girl who was clumsy, dizzy, and untrustworthy with scissors may grow to be a more self-aware and functional teenager.

The next stories suggest that occupational therapy can bring about dramatic changes in adolescents' and adults' lives, too. As you'll see from the following accounts of individuals who were treated after childhood, the experience of OT can be freeing.

NEW BODY MAP
MARLENE GOMEZ

I managed to survive adolescence, did better in college, and began working with children with autism.

When I was twenty-three, my supervisor one day turned to me and said the magic words, "You have sensory issues." Her visionary perception of what made me, well...me, changed my life forever. I went into the master's program for OT and started learning about sensory integration.

It had a name! It was something! Most of all, it had a solution! I didn't have to just cope; I could actually change how I felt, how I interacted with the world!

After applying to myself the principles I was using to treat children, I started eating a wider variety of foods, got less aggressive toward people, less hyperalert. I could drive without crashing (I used to crash at least two times every six months!), wear wool, and be touched.

I had just been in constant search of being in sync, in a never-ending quest to stay safe, in balance, and attuned. Learning I was not crazy, traumatized, stupid, or evil was the fundamental step. It made me change my perception and reevaluate my life process.

I learned to watch a person's movement, body symmetry, and muscle tension to know where proprioception might be impaired. As an adolescent or adult, learning a new body map is achieved through active awareness, unlike the way a child learns about his body through play. The "magic" trick to creating a new and rich body map is not just doing exercise; it is becoming aware of what you are moving, how you move, and your body position. Breathing, yoga, meditation, and slow, sustained movement are tools to get the body and mind functioning as one, instead of as disconnected entities.

Even without therapy, it is possible to cope with SPD symptoms, complete a college career, and exist. But if you want more than just survival, therapy is needed. The feeling of being in tune, even if not as constant as for non-SPD people, is worth the effort of putting yourself through the work of relearning your body and rewiring your brain. Because then, it will get better. Happiness, life quality, and freedom will be your reward.

SENSE OF PURPOSE
KYLIE BOAZMAN

After being diagnosed at fifteen, I was unhappy and worried about my future. Everything I had read emphasized the importance of early intervention for best results, and it was relatively rare that someone who was diagnosed as an adolescent or adult would seek treatment.

My parents were doing research as well and looking for support from family and friends. Another parent suggested occupational therapy to help me understand my diagnosis and deal with depression. The therapist, Angie Voss (author of *Your Essential Guide to Understanding Sensory Processing Disorder*), admitted that she had limited experience working with teenagers, but agreed to begin seeing me. I attended classes for part of the day and left midway to visit her. This routine gave me a scheduled break from academic work, and after OT, I could return to school happier, relaxed, and refocused for the rest of the day.

OT was like nothing I had ever experienced, and I think having such an amazing therapist made the difference. Angie would explain to me what she wanted to try, such as:

- Using a "cuddle swing" for spinning deep pressure
- Rolling weighted balls on my back and limbs
- Trying weighted blankets and clothing
- Playing with toys with different textures
- Throwing heavy balls back and forth

In between different parts of the session, she would ask me how I was feeling and what was going on in my head and body before returning to focusing on sensory activities. Her skillful therapy was so subtle, and I felt so much better while I was there, that I didn't notice the questions or how my coping mechanisms were changing.

OT had several immediate benefits, and it also taught me a lot that I still carry with me. For instance, Angie encouraged me to take on more of a leadership role in my school's service learning organization, which I had been active in for many years. Focusing on helping others and developing long-term projects gave me a sense of purpose and a comfortable environment that was neither school nor home.

One of the takeaway lessons of OT-SI was the importance of self-care. I needed to know how to alleviate my stress, cope with overwhelming situations, and implement different practices into my day as preventive care. What I developed with my therapist was essentially a toolkit for everyday life and emergencies.[4]

I know that when other people are diagnosed later than in childhood, they also look for resources and information everywhere. Although many recent publications emphasize early intervention, teenagers and adults can still benefit from occupational therapy in immediate and long-term ways.

---

4   Kylie's *physical* toolkit includes items such as hand fidgets and weighted blankets, for her room, bag, and car. Her *conceptual* toolkit is a plan of self-awareness to help her establish routines and be prepared for unexpected situations. (Her toolkit ideas are included among the coping tips listed at the end of several chapters in this book.)

IT'S NEVER TOO LATE
MEREDITH JOSEPH BLAINE

In my midtwenties, I found out that I had SPD. I was whisked into a huge sensory gym with swings, gymnastic balls, scooter boards, and all kinds of enticing toys and equipment that children would have a ball with. My therapist had me play with all those things, just like a kid.

You know what? I had so much fun with OT-SI!

As a kid at heart, I still crave fun movement and physical activity. I get a rush from roller coasters, get a splash out of water parks, and love to cut loose at gymnastics facilities, tumbling, climbing, and bouncing. Today, my sensory lifestyle has developed into one that combines playful activities, to satisfy these kidlike cravings, with more "grown-up" activities, like pushing shopping carts and vacuum cleaners.

If you suspect that you have SPD, please don't be afraid to consult with a sensory-trained occupational therapist. If you are found to have SPD, you and your OT should talk about how to meet your sensory needs and develop a sensory lifestyle. This can be as simple as increasing everyday physical activities such as pushing, pulling, lifting, and carrying and, if need be, oral activities like chewing, sucking, and/or blowing. There's absolutely nothing wrong with gardening, housekeeping, or lifting weights.

All adolescents and adults—who either grew up with their SPD or have recently been diagnosed—need to find many different ways to help them cope with SPD and function better as human, social beings. If you feel uncomfortable in a gym designed for young children, don't hesitate to voice your concern. Your therapist will respect your wishes and help develop your sensory strategies while maintaining your dignity.

But if you are a newly diagnosed teenager or young adult and you walk into a sensory gym and feel like you have just died and gone to a fun and playful heaven, more power to you! You'll love jumping on trampolines and bouncing around... and around... on hopping balls (gymnastic balls with a handle). These activities are fun and also great work for your core and coordination, as well as for cardio fitness and lymphatic health. Your therapist will suggest ways to extend those playful experiences (as long as they are more or less socially accept-able) outside the gym. Amazing, isn't it?

When you do get OT-SI, I sincerely hope, if you are married or have a significant other, that the special one in your life can understand your special needs as a "sensory kid, all grown up." I hope your special one can be open-minded enough to share not only your experiences, but also the fun that you may crave, love, and require.

Now is a good time to be evaluated and to deal with SPD in what-ever way you feel comfortable. It's never too late!

This next story turns to another kind of treatment—orthodontia. Kevin describes his relief and satisfaction when he was treated with compassion in the dentist's chair. What a difference it makes when a doctor or therapist can say, "I truly feel your pain—and know how to make things better."

MY BRACES BUDDY
KEVIN LARSON

A terrible overbite and really sore gums meant I needed braces. This is taken in stride by many people, but not for somebody with sensory is-sues. I hate having people's hands in my mouth; I can't stand latex gloves; and I don't like surprises.

The first two orthodontists were horrible. They were in such a hurry to progress and wanted to shove trays of goop in my mouth to make impressions during my first or second visit. There was no way I could handle that! I felt like I was choking to death, with my mom watching! The orthodontists would get really frustrated and mad when I pushed their hands away.

After these miserable attempts, we found a very helpful orthodontist who has a young son with autism. He was patient and calm and sensitive to my needs. He did everything he could to make orthodontia tolerable.

Since I'm a gagger, he actually allowed me to make impressions on his teeth, while his eyes watered and he tried not to gag. On the first attempt, he took the tray out early on purpose and showed me that the imprints of his teeth were sloppy and needed more time to set up. So he had me redo them, and this time he left the trays in the entire time necessary while he struggled not to gag. Then we went to his lab to make a plaster model of his teeth, which was totally cool. The good impression made a nice, clear model. (I got to keep it!) He gave my mom a container of the impression stuff and some trays, mirrors, and such, so we could practice at home. I made impressions of my fingers, some pennies, little toys, and even of my own front teeth.

Then the time came to make the real impressions. After several tries, during multiple office visits, he figured out that if he used less than the required amount of water to mix it up, the goop wouldn't ooze as much, but since it would set up much faster, he had to move really quickly. So, as I stood beside him at the sink and watched, he mixed up a batch, and before I knew what he was doing, he stepped behind me, reached around, moved my jaw down with his thumb, and popped the tray of goop right into my mouth. He stood for a few seconds, holding it in my mouth, talking calmly and quietly, with his other arm holding me tight against him, and quickly, it was done! He took the tray out and saw that it was a good impression, and it was all over. He was so quick that I stayed relaxed. Hooray! Success!

My advice to other people with tactile overresponsivity is to keep searching until they find one who pays attention to their needs. And I wish that all dentists were trained to understand people with autism and sensory issues, as my "Braces Buddy" does.

Every teenager would feel lucky to receive treatment from a professional who is familiar with sensory difficulties and curious to learn more . . . who uses art and science to try new techniques . . . who has the interest and time to listen to clients, ask what they need, and explain what's happening, so the procedures are not surprising or scary . . . and who relates to each patient as a person, not just another malocclusion.

Not only specialists, but also we parents, teachers, and other nonprofessionals, can observe adolescents' behavior and what experiences are not going well. Then we can do something. We can provide on-the-spot treatment, which is often as simple as removing offending sensations and providing useful ones instead.

For example, as an unseasoned music and movement teacher, I noticed that when I brought out the rhythm band basket, about 15 percent of the preschoolers would clap their hands over their ears, curl up, and cry. I knew nothing then about auditory overresponsivity, but I knew not to torture my students. Their misery was mystifying. Why couldn't the agitated ones just calm down, and the droopy ones just rev up? Why couldn't these out-of-sync kids just have fun, like everyone else?

I started watching their responses when I lightly tapped the cymbals and triangle, twitched the tambourine, and jiggled the jingle bells. The ear clappers hated these sounds, although I played *pianississimo* (very softly).

My investigation continued. I tapped rhythm sticks, rubbed a guiro (a notched gourd) with a wooden stick, beat a tom-tom, shook a maraca, and rotated a bamboo rain stick filled with tiny pebbles.

These were sounds that did not seem to bother the defensive children. In fact, they leaned in to watch and listen and then chose these instruments to pick up and play.

Aha! The difference was that the Not OK sounds were metallic; the OK sounds were wood, leather, gourds, seeds, and pebbles. Although clueless then about the theory of sensory integration, I deduced that bright, jangling, high-frequency sounds caused physical pain. Beating rhythms with softer, organic, low-frequency sound makers was much more pleasant. I banished the metal instruments to a high shelf.

When you take away something of value, you must replace it with something of equal value. So we started making instruments to replenish the basket. We spent extra time outside searching for natural materials to "play." Thus evolved our Environmental Rhythm Band, with percussive instruments made from sticks, dried leaves, pinecones, seedpods, acorns, and stones. My "treatment" made a difference. I saw and heard children change, and the noises we made now were joyful indeed.

As an added benefit, the process of building a collection of percussive instruments engaged seven senses. (Not gustatory—we didn't lick them.) The end result was more attuned children and happier music class.

How does this story relate to older kids? Well, the lesson I learned working with young children is applicable to people at any age.

When we stop, look, and listen, we can become good detectives. Observations about what sensations are Not OK and what treatments bring relief can lead to simple yet helpful change at home or school.

AT HOME IN HEADPHONES
KEVIN LARSON

My mom has sensory issues, too, so she understands. Sometimes she and I escape together. What we need is a soundproof room in our house. We could go in there, or send the noisy people in there!

Since we don't have a soundproof room, I use noise-canceling headphones when it all gets to be too much. When my little brother's playing with his squeaky, clicky Transformers, Mom and Dad listen to music I hate, we go to see fireworks, or something stupid is on TV, I use them. That way, other people don't have to stop what they're doing, and I'm comfortable. Sometimes, after a youth group meeting or a loud social event, I wear them home in the car with my eyes closed, just to decompress for a while before I have to spend time with people again. Putting on those headphones really gives me a chance to rest when I'm wiped out and makes it all just go away.

Most people, with or without SPD, come up with some form of self-therapy to stay in a state of homeostasis. To get the brain and body synchronized, we may lift weights, swim laps, knead bread, chew gum, or make music. To relax, a book or a bath may be exactly what we need.

Some of the young people I've spoken with admit that they've tried smoking, drinking, drugs, speeding on motorcycles, and wild, dangerous experiences to dull the pain produced by living with SPD in a perplexing world. Teenagers with sensory underresponsivity may sporadically seek strong sensation to rev up and get in sync. Sensory cravers may seek maximum sensory stimulation around the clock. (During puberty, ordinary neurological changes in the brain compel typical teenagers to seek new and exciting sensations. Add SPD to the mix and you may have a recipe for risky thrills.)

A MOTORCYCLE'S SOOTHING SOUNDS
PAUL BALIUS

I love the sound of machines. Though bad sounds can be very bad, a soothing, comforting sound that masks the bad sounds can be very good. Driving in cars can be hard for me with certain rattling noises. I prefer to be on my loud motorcycle where the sound is very high, but the noise is pleasurable. I started riding a motorcycle when I was seventeen. I never felt any sensory pain, never felt as free as I was when I was riding. It gave me a sense of freedom from being around others.

The real grit of riding is eating bugs, getting nailed with little rocks kicked up by trucks, and dealing with extreme weather at the speed of Hold-On-Tight! You will never smell the sweet aroma of spring locked in a car or room. For me, the pain of weather and rocks is nothing, small annoyances, and for these small things I trade the agony of normal sounds. (Note: I never encourage anyone to ride motorcycles, as they can be very dangerous.)

LOVED A GOOD MOSH PIT!
LAURIE APPEL

Weird, awkward, and super shy, I found very unhealthy ways to cope throughout my adolescence and young adulthood. Drugs, alcohol, and loud heavy metal music became my escape. I loved a good mosh pit! I remember going to concerts and putting my head in the speakers, craving the vibration in an attempt to numb the pain of words constantly being spoken at me.

While Laurie Appel was growing up, she craved intense sensory experiences. She didn't want to be as far away as possible from the crowd and the audio speakers; she wanted to be inside them! Today, Laurie fully understands how to address sensory needs in a more appropriate way. In her OT clinic, she offers not a mosh pit but, instead, a multisensory ball pit—a padded "pond" filled with small, colorful balls—to alert or calm her clients' sensory systems. She gets in it herself, naturally, because some things don't change.

Every one of us has particular sensory preferences. Where some love turbulence, others love calm. One size doesn't fit all, so find the safe, simple solutions that are right for you.

SENSORY DETOXIFICATION
CHLOE ROTHSCHILD

I have to reduce the overload in me, and sometimes it can be very hard or not even possible. I may have to lie on my bed, covered by my weighted blanket, with the lights off and my mini fan on, since I like the white noise that sounds from it, and I like it blowing on me, 'cause I like that feeling. Then I type on my laptop, as that is a very calming activity. I like to refer to this as sensory detoxification!

SQUARE HOLES
LYDIA WAYMAN

From a young age, I have always felt like a square peg in a round hole. I have lived in a world too bright, too harsh, too loud, too everything. Tights made my legs feel like my skin was peeling off. The most comfortable shoes in the store rubbed blisters into my feet. I would eat only a handful of foods, and others made me gag and throw up on the spot. Too much, it was . . . or rather, is. It's still too much.

Thankfully, I've learned coping strategies, mostly on my own, by trial and error. A purring cat, some good exercise, or just a long nap generally sets my system to rights. Writing and typing are the means by which I process the world around me, the way that I sync my senses, my thoughts, and my actions. I've learned ways to explain to other people what it's like in my head. For example, when I speak, I'm really just reading aloud what I have mentally typed out.

It is known that many people with autism also have SPD, and I would argue that SPD is at the root of some people's autism. It is for me.

Somewhere along the way, I realized that by making myself a comfortable space in which to exist in this world, and by doing a bit of self-advocating, I've essentially constructed for myself a square-hole drill. Square holes, for me and all the other square pegs in the world, are long overdue.

Through professional therapy or one's own explorations, "square pegs" can find coping strategies to help them make getting through the day easier.

CHAPTER 13

Nurturing Your Passion

Everyone is born with the inner drive to be a "doer," not a "do-ee." To do is to express oneself through words or actions. To do is to develop into a self-governing human being.

Human development is entwined with sensory processing. You may remember reading in chapter 2, "Primer," about four essential functions of sensory processing: defensiveness or self-protection (for survival); discrimination (for learning); action (for participating in daily life); and satisfaction (for feeling good).

In this chapter, we'll take a closer look at these four functions. We'll hear from individuals with SPD who are working hard to overcome sensory problems at school and work, to gain knowledge and learn new skills, to participate in life and contribute to society, and to feel good—physically, emotionally, and intellectually. We'll see that pursuing a passion, whether for an activity or a larger cause, can fuel our need to "do" and make even the most challenging efforts worthwhile.

PRACTICE, PRACTICE, PRACTICE
KARLY KOOP

"One...two...three...Jump!"

Nothing happened.

"One...two...three...Jump!"

Hmmm...Nothing happened, again.

I know I can jump off this four-inch-tall step, but every time I try, my legs and feet stay on the curb...and then I try again and again. It has been like this all my life. My brain knows exactly what my body should do. I can describe it, picture it, and coach someone else to do it, but my body doesn't always do what my brain knows. I have motor planning issues—dyspraxia.

Dyspraxia is like this: Take a pen and put it between the toes of your left foot. Now write your name in cursive. See! Your brain knows exactly how to do that, but good luck getting your foot to make it happen. After lots and lots of practice, you can do it. After lots more practice, you might be good at it!

I have probably practiced simple motor skills more hours than most athletes practice to perfect their sports skills. Simple things like walking, kneeling, and jumping don't come easy. As a kid, I broke twelve bones doing things like running and riding a bike. My muscles didn't get the hint that I was falling, so when I fell, I fell with a splat. The best advice my mom got was to let me do whatever I felt I could do— not to coddle or protect me from falling. If I broke something, the doctor would patch me up, and we'd go on. Falling down never stopped me!

When I decided to play basketball, I stood in the driveway for hours tossing the ball to the basket...and missing. We later discovered that I have visual processing issues. But, at the time, I slowly figured out exactly where to shoot the ball to make it go in the basket. I appear to aim about three feet left of the basket but consistently sink the shot. I may be unable to hold my own against the quick and aggressive girls on the basketball court, but I'm awesome in my driveway!

Then I got hooked on karate. I am a third-degree brown belt, thanks to patient people who are just as determined to teach me as I am to learn. Karate has turned out to be the best physical therapy and has made a huge difference in my motor planning, my strength, and especially my confidence. I even won the "Warrior Spirit Award" for my determination and courage.

My school years have been both tough and wonderful. I have to work really hard. The homework I turn in doesn't much look like what everyone else does, but it looks good to me. I am not socially up to par with the rest of the kids, and, boy, do they know how to find my weak spots! There are a lot of mean kids out there.

One of the brightest times has been dance class. Yes, dance class! Freshman year, I took Pom Squad, and the drill team/dance teachers fell in love with me and "adopted" me. In fact, they invited me to be in their dance classes! No one had ever invited me to do something that requires huge amounts of motor skills. These teachers taught me to dance. They stretched my muscles beyond what anyone thought possible and taught me to pirouette, leap, roll, and do all kinds of complicated moves. They have loved, encouraged, and believed in me and have been my refuge in high school.

One really cool thing about my motor and visual difficulties is that I "see" things differently and figure out new ways to get things done. For instance, I taught a little neighbor to ride her bike after her parents gave up. We practiced every day for two weeks. One day, holding on to the trainer bar on the back of the bike, I had an idea. I told the girl to let her back touch the bar. She did that and took off riding on her own! She just needed to feel the security of that bar to know she wouldn't fall. No one else saw that bar as anything but a handle for the adult to use to help balance. But it made sense to me to use the bar like a back on a chair, so she could get tactile and proprioceptive input to help her balance.

My mom says that I have the unique ability to see everyone as exactly the same—equal in all ways—because I have always seen myself that way. It doesn't matter if someone relies on a wheelchair or is captain of the football team. This gives me an advantage when being around kids who have special needs. I spent one afternoon working with a teacher who has an autistic student. This student worked with me, doing things he had never done for his teacher. It was amazing! He knew that I accept him just the way he is and that my whole purpose was to be with him and help him.

Being "out of sync" with the rest of the world isn't such a bad thing. In fact, I think it's a blessing—it's what makes me . . . me. I like the way I am, and I appreciate that my uniqueness can help other kids. I am graduating from high school in a few weeks, and I am excited to see how I can use this gift to make a difference for other people.

Karly's attitude about having dyspraxia is awe inspiring. Imagine what this young woman will achieve with her determination and spirit!

Karly's story echoes Shonda's: School is hard; relationships are few and far between; self-esteem is low. Ah, but when these young women learn to dance, their dyspraxia seems to disappear. What helps them are supportive teachers, the rhythm and cadence of the music, the framework and repetition of the dance routine, the utter joy of movement, and their own extrasensory grace.

Every person has gifts. Gifts need time and space and nurturing to grow. In the next stories, we'll see how music and movement can help young people with SPD feel more in sync and get in the groove, allowing them to overcome limitations and nourish their passion. In addition to being fulfilling and fun, the just-right activity can be transformative.

A DRUMMER AT HEART
MICHAEL JACOBS

I am a drummer at heart, but many years ago, few would have believed that. I am also living proof that with inner drive and the proper guidance, people with challenges can overcome academic, social, and emotional obstacles that SPD presents.

Throughout elementary school, I had severe sensory problems and very few friends. I couldn't attend music class because the sounds of the piano and my classmates' singing overwhelmed me. After much encouragement and therapy, I was finally able to join in with my classmates playing the recorder. To everyone's surprise, I could play every song in the book on the very first day. Then I tried the snare drum in the concert band. I loved it but quit after two weeks because I was progressing much faster than the other kids and became bored and disruptive.

In middle school, my desire to learn the drums resurfaced. My mother hired a private drum instructor. Soon, my new teacher said I was "gifted" with music. I made the jazz band, learned to love performing, and started to make many friends. Music had given me the huge social boost I needed.

When I entered high school, my parents forced me to join the marching band. They knew I wouldn't join any other club, and they insisted that I be involved in something besides academics. Luckily my ambition and talent helped me to make the bass drum, which every high school drummer wants to play, instead of cymbals. I was the only freshman to do this.

After the first day of drumline, I set two goals: one, to make the snare drum the next year and two, to become the drum captain my senior year. At our first pep rally of my senior year, I was introduced to the whole student body as this year's drum captain. It was an unbelievable feeling hearing everyone cheer for me, their classmate and friend!

As drum captain I now have the opportunity to help others. Being a leader in a nationally known marching band of 331 students isn't something that my young self thought would be possible. My journey with music has taught me that I can accomplish my dreams with hard work, perseverance, and belief in myself. This lesson has shaped who I am and will continue to shape who I will ultimately become.

And, yes, I have thanked my parents.

SINGING MEANS EVERYTHING TO ME
EMBER WALKER

As a girl, I often couldn't sleep at night because I could hear every little creak in the house and my sister breathing loudly across the room. Even the bugs outside seemed like they all had their own megaphones. In my family I am known as the "Bat" for being able to hear a pin drop in the other room.

However, I have found solace and the positive in some of my struggles. Like, "bat hearing" became my friend when, still in junior high, I was able to make the high school show choir. In my small town, this achievement was unheard of. Music became my life, and singing means everything to me. Now, I sing for friends and family, and I even get paid to sing when requested!

Michael's leading the drumline and Ember's becoming a singer are great examples of how music can be a lifeline for people with sensory issues. One reason for this is that music tends to restore order. Another reason is that people who are very sensitive in a *negative* way to loud, random noises may be very sensitive in a *positive* and expressive way to rhythm, pitch, and harmony. Even if they can't sing or play an instrument, they frequently have an extrasensory affinity for music.

Many young people with SPD, such as Karly, earlier, and Paul, next, love martial arts. Judo, tae kwon do, and karate help them feel strong, satisfied, and accomplished. Meanwhile, others revel in the great outdoors.

MARTIAL ARTS: WHERE I BELONGED
PAUL BALIUS

At twenty, I joined a martial arts school. There I found such peace! The physical activity and discipline were so influential on my life. I never had pain there. It was not a team sport, so finally I found somewhere that I belonged in my aloneness. The hard exercise relieved so much stress. I loved every aspect—the meditation, standing on my head, doing the precision body movements—I even enjoyed sparring. I spent several years doing this, and it helped me transition from a teenager to a young man. To this day I can see the influence it had on my life.

I LOVE THE SENSATION OF FALLING THROUGH SPACE
TYLER ANN WHITNEY

I am a sensory kid. At least, that is what my mom, an occupational therapy assistant, calls me. I'm a sensory craver, which means that I find sensory input all by myself. I am constantly swinging, flipping, or bending over backward. I especially like and need a lot of vestibular input.

When I was younger, I didn't get OT but my parents used to brush my limbs, and the deep pressure felt so good! I also had a chewy tube, which is a safe thing to chew on that stimulates oral and proprioceptive input.

I do very well in school and on the high school softball team. At school, when I am supposed to be sitting down like everyone else, I am usually sitting with my feet under me, or just squatting with my feet on the chair. At home, I rest on the floor with my knees under me to do my homework.

I like jumping on the trampoline, stretching, sports, and martial arts. I love doing fun outdoorsy things, like camping, hiking, rock climbing and rappelling. I am a thrill seeker. At the Grand Canyon, I jumped off a forty-foot waterfall several times because I love the sensation of falling through space.

Camping one night, we made a bonfire and swung over it on a rope swing. You could feel the heat as your body passed over the flame. Cool! The next morning we played on long zip lines. To brake, you wear thick gloves and squeeze the rope. Well, I was going so fast that I couldn't slow down, so I crashed into the man who was waiting for me. I escaped with only minor cuts and bruises . . . He died (kidding!).

Although I am living with a sensory processing disorder, I am doing just fine. It is fun to explain to your friends why you are acting like a child even though you are a teenager. Like I said, I am a sensory kid!

Having SPD can also inspire adolescents or young adults to enter a professional field that otherwise may not have interested them. Occupational therapy, advocacy for people with developmental differences, mentoring foster parents, working with visually impaired children, and mental health counseling are examples. Here is a story about becoming an optometrist.

THE OUT-OF-SYNC EYE DOCTOR
CHARLES SHIDLOFSKY, OD, FCOVD

I was the out-of-sync child before we knew what an out-of-sync child was. I remember my mother buying nice pants or a suit for me, and I would walk around stiff-legged so that I would not have to touch the sides of the pants because of tactile overresponsivity. My blue jeans had to be washed at least a dozen times before I would wear them. My auditory processing was acute; I lived near a major airport and could tell you the type of airplane flying overhead by the sound of the jet engines.

Of course, in school this was a major distraction. When I was reading, my eyes would tear up after about twenty minutes, words would move on the page, and eventually I would fall asleep. School was a major frustration. No matter how hard I worked, getting an A in a class was an elusive concept although I was working harder than my peers.

My fine motor and gross motor skills were definitely limited. My handwriting was awful, as I could not stay on the line, and my spacing was very asymmetrical. My grip on the pen or pencil was very tight, and my hand would hurt after a short time. I was very uncoordinated, and sports was another area that was difficult, particularly in elementary school.

Thankfully, I have this personality quirk called perseverance. If you tell me that I am not capable of doing something, I will work exceedingly hard to prove you wrong.

One can see that my visual, auditory, proprioceptive, vestibular, and kinesthetic systems were affected by SPD. Unfortunately, this was never recognized. My parents took me for psychological testing as a young teenager to find out why my schoolwork was not living up to my IQ. The psychologists said that I was capable—but probably not working hard enough.

I managed to do well enough in school to get into a good university. But I felt that something must be wrong with how I learn because I was working so hard yet only able to get mediocre grades. I had to take some actions to improve (and survive). I had to find something that interested me so much that I could push through and work hard enough to be successful.

During my freshman year, I realized that I was having a hard time seeing the board in the large lecture halls. I went to the eye doctor and got my first pair of glasses. Every few months after that, I was back in his office to get a stronger prescription. The more I went, the more intrigued I became with the profession of optometry. At the end of my sophomore year, I decided that optometry was what I wanted to pursue.

During my first year at the college of optometry, I was diagnosed with convergence insufficiency.¹ I began therapy to help my eyes work better as a team and learned as much as I could. When I started in practice, I began to integrate vision therapy into my general eye care practice. I took what I learned in school and added techniques I developed on my own (I was my own first patient) to develop a highly successful vision therapy program that I use to this day.

Of course, I am constantly tweaking the program and making it better. I look within and outside our field to further understand binocular vision problems and other learning-related vision problems. I work closely with occupational therapists, physical therapists, psychologists, physicians, speech pathologists, etc., to integrate what we all are doing to help patients. This integrated approach to care is so important to our patients' success.

As you can see, I was the Out-of-Sync Child, the Out-of-Sync Student, and the Out-of-Sync Eye Doctor. In many ways, being out of sync

---

1 Convergence insufficiency, a common yet often overlooked visual problem, occurs when your eyes don't turn inward as they should while you try to focus on a close object. This sensory and neuromuscular problem hinders binocular vision (using both eyes to see one image).

helped me by keeping me open-minded to look at new ideas, new therapies, or more traditional therapies in a new light. I love what I do—it is both my job and my hobby. My main goal every day is to make children and adults not have to go through what I went through to learn. I want to make that process easier so they can have more success in school, in work, and in life.

A similar spark to do work that benefits others has also inspired Kerry Magro (the boy who ate only bologna). Despite an occasional tendency to lose his balance or to lose his nerve, Kerry doesn't see obstacles; instead, he sees opportunities to keep moving forward.

THE FIRE TO FIGHT
KERRY MAGRO

"Do not fall! Keep your balance!" As I rise to speak to a crowd today, that's the voice I hear in my head. It encapsulates all the sensory issues I have experienced since being diagnosed at four with PDD-NOS[2] and SPD. At twenty-five I'm able to travel the country alone to discuss my experiences and advocate for people with disabilities. I have thrived because of family support, multiple therapies, and personal motivation.

Today I realized that in order not to shut down when speaking, I need a lot more self-regulation. The overstimulating lights, the noise from the microphones, and being up on stage remind me about sensory issues I can finally deal with and issues I still need help on. Grow-

---

2 PDD-NOS is pervasive developmental disorder, not otherwise specified. This diagnosis is a common one for individuals on the autism spectrum and pertains to severe impairment in social interaction, communication, and/or stereotyped behavior.

ing up, I learned that sensory issues don't go away but do become manageable when I'm aware of them.

When I was younger, auditory, tactile, and vestibular challenges interfered with daily life. My mother says that as a family, while we may have found a way to live with my diagnoses, none of us could live with my SPD. It impeded our family's functioning and had to be resolved, if I was to move forward.

Auditory and tactile issues have lessened but vestibular issues still get in my way. As a kid, I was fearful of falling, but poor coordination made me fall constantly. I was frightened to have my feet off the ground or to walk on "mushy" surfaces, including grass and sand. My mother loved the beach and, regrettably, vacationing at the shore was not part of our family life with me around.

What helped, first, was acknowledging the problem and not expecting that I'd grow out of it. And second, countless occupational therapy sessions at home, school, and the clinic.

OT-SI was most important to my success in living independently. Therapists addressed my dyspraxia by increasing my sensory experiences and tolerances through messy play activities. We cornered the Gak[3] market, as well. We worked on my hypersensitivity to movement and problems knowing where my body was in space. I took piano lessons for fine motor coordination and chess to learn to take turns. I learned to balance while alternating feet so I didn't have to bump downstairs on my rump. I became able to take my feet off the ground enough to swing in a playground. Eventually, I could ride elevators and tolerate flying, although I don't enjoy it much.

What happened to the little boy with so little internal regulation that he wanted only to play by himself? With therapy and a lot of hard work, my coordination greatly improved. In high school, I could dribble

---

3   Gak: Squeezable, stretchable molding substance for children's play.

a ball well enough to play basketball. I still lack upper body strength but mastered bowling with a lot of practice. Riding a bike is on my "bucket list" of life goals. I still need to use noise-canceling headphones and earplugs and do not like to get dirty or messy—but I do go to the beach occasionally.

So, even though I used to fall, that time is in the past. My main difficulty now is nerves. When I first started public speaking and the nerves kicked in, my balance suffered. I'd shake, talk too fast, blurt out many "um's" and "uh's," fidget and rock, and make awkward gestures.

In graduate school, I found methods to control my nerves. I learned to center my mind on specific topics I was passionate about as well as make use of muscle memory. I turned my passion for advocacy for the disabled community into a tool to conquer my nerves and their undesirable effects. From writing out my speeches on a computer, working on lower body exercises, and practicing in a mirror, I was soon on my way. Pronouncing also helped me tremendously. I've also trained to make eye contact with people, which takes effort but is achievable and so very important for a speaker.

Giving a recent speech in my hometown—one of the first times I told a group that I was on the autism spectrum—I was still terrified. Despite that, I used the moment as a learning experience, a therapy, to move myself forward.

The best advice I can offer anyone with a hurdle big or small is: Never be afraid to acknowledge your problems, work hard to overcome them, and self-advocate to get support. Stretch yourself to become comfortable with your weaknesses. Even if they never become strengths, you will be a much better person for fighting always. Nothing is better than having the fire to fight! It gives you the ability to strive.

I have found a way to manage successfully. That's what I want for everyone!

Kerry wants to light the way for all young people like him to achieve their goals. Along with many other speakers in this book, Kerry is my hero. A hero, according to Joseph Campbell, the renowned scholar of mythology and religion, is one with exceptional inner drive who feels compelled to do something extraordinarily important. The hero "ventures forth from the world of common day," meets formidable forces, is victorious . . . and then returns, empowered with wisdom and skills to benefit other human beings.

Many of the young heroes in this book give their lives to something bigger than themselves. This something may be writing or speaking about differences, motivating little kids to ride bikes, or being a friend to others in need. It may be composing music, dancing and singing, creating art, or sharing recipes. Doing what they want to do, can do, must do, they are "following their bliss."

The heroes and heroines in these pages still struggle with sensory issues, because only rarely does one completely grow out of SPD; one grows into it and learns how to cope with it. However, SPD does not deter these courageous, generous-hearted young adults. Rather, it inspires them to use their special sensitivity to follow their bliss, to go through new doors and to be present, to make things better—to do.

DO IT!

Paul Balius

Set out objectives that you desire in your heart to do in your life. Do not live a life of unrealized potential. Swap in a great adventure of something you can do to replace a type of experience that you cannot tolerate.

Read about people who share in your condition and can understand you.

Be willing to give someone else the very thing you need so much yourself.

Meet others like yourself. Find someone safe you can talk to. Write about yourself. Communicate to others what you like or dislike.

Accept your condition but do not accept limitations. If you have a bad experience, do not necessarily make this something you will not ever do again. Do not be embittered for what you cannot do. Instead, be emboldened to do more than you ever thought was possible.

To change your life, try this idea, the Monthly Triple Play. This is where you change three things every month.

1. Pick something that you need to stop. We all have these! Pick something small at first, so you can develop your confidence in your ability to change yourself.
2. Pick something you want to start. We all have something we need to start! Keep it small at first, but whatever you choose, do it!
3. Think of a relationship that you need to repair or restore. Start with an easy one, like reconnecting with someone you like or getting back in touch with a relative.

Do not accept the idea that you are alone; you are not alone. Know that there are plenty of people who have struggled during their adolescence, too—people who know what it is like for you now, who believe in you.

Keep striving. Stay hopeful. You are a wonderfully unique you. You are the most powerful change agent of you.

You can improve your life. Do it!

CHAPTER 14

Moving into Adulthood with SPD

On the whole, the contributors to this book are positive thinkers. Generally, they have grown and changed; the worst is past, and the best is yet to be.

Informed now, they know and can anticipate the specific sensory stimuli (or lack of sensory stimuli) that make them feel out of sync. They have learned some sensory strategies to get in sync, on the spot. Some have learned to appreciate SPD as a gift. Named and tamed, SPD is no longer an inscrutable and unbeatable monster.

Near the beginning of this book is a list of common questions that parents ask about their children. One question is, "Does everything turn out all right in the end?" Many contributors say that, yes, it can, as children grow.

Growing up not only enables but also drives many teenagers to take responsibility for coping with sensory challenges. They *must* take responsibility if they hope to become independent—and Mom, Dad, or Favorite OT won't always be there to help during a sensory meltdown, anyway. Even when maturation comes slowly, adolescents gradually learn to take ownership of their SPD and to develop new strengths and abilities.

MOVING FORWARD AND STAYING PATIENT

Rachel S. Schneider

In terms of ownership, a diagnosis of SPD in teenagehood is split between the teen and parent. Not entirely responsible for their ultimate well-being, but too aware to be completely disengaged, SPD teens don't always take the lead in their diagnosis and treatment. I've spoken to many parents who can't figure out a way to rouse their sensory teen into ownership and don't feel comfortable taking complete ownership of the diagnosis themselves. This means that for some teens, their sensory symptoms—heightened by the hormonal surge and internal sensitivities—fall quietly into an untended chasm. Unchecked, sensitivities get worse and even become engulfing. Questions are asked about how they'll survive a school club meeting, let alone college.

This is who I was in my late teens—undiagnosed and unsure of myself and my differences. In some ways, I was ultimately successful. Still unaware of the root cause of my anxiety, I finished high school within the somewhat narrow parameters of my difficulties. I went to college and was on my own for the first time. I jumped from social situation to social situation, trying each to see what fit and felt comfortable. Instead of experimenting with substances (why bother when many days with SPD feel like a bad trip?), I experimented with my abilities: Could I tolerate a concert? Sometimes, in smaller venues, if I was feeling well that day. Could I handle a big party? Maybe, if I stood with my friends in the corner and left before I felt completely drained. I laughed and went for homemade ice cream, hosted movie nights, and lay with my friends under budding trees, studying. I graduated a year early, eager to return to my more familiar, more contained life.

Teenagehood is a temporary state of transition from childhood to adulthood. It is a strange time of change and movement into the unknown. We are suddenly more aware of our place in the world, and yet we are peering out at the larger world safely from the familiar confines of home and family. We can almost touch who we'll be and how we'll handle the future, but not quite.

In an SPD teenagehood, I would argue that success lies in the survival—in the maintaining and even thriving—of one's self in spite of the issues of hormonal flux, ownership of sensory challenges, parental acceptance, and self-understanding. It's in the moving forward and the staying patient. It's in the willingness to believe that the hormonal haze will clear, the unfamiliar will be revealed. And in the transfer of the reins of personal responsibility from parents and guardians, a stronger sensory self will appear.

—From Rachel Schneider's blog, *The Sensational Struggle and Success of SPD Teenagers*, March 2015

It does turn out all right when adolescents gain new coping skills, and (from what OTs and parents have told me) especially when their families are right there with them, cheering them on.

SOMETHING PRETTY SPECIAL
ANNETTE HIMMELREICH

SPD is not a disorder to me anymore. Part of my success is helping parents to understand and accept their child's situation and help them cope with SPD and turn it into a victory rather than a deficit. Their child can be successful when given understanding, encouragement, and most of all, love. Parents need to know the ability to cope with SPD can form a child into something pretty special.

Could it be that having SPD can raise adolescents to higher levels of self-awareness than their typical peers develop? Could SPD open the door for a more intense way of experiencing the world? Could being determined to overcome adversity—every day!—make the teenager with SPD braver and stronger? Could SPD be considered a gift? Some individuals who have grown up with it certainly think so.

PREPARED TO EXCEL
KEVIN LARSON

Here's what is good about having SPD: I get to see life from a unique perspective. It would be so boring to be normal! I can usually help people see things from a different angle, which makes them think differently. My visual acuity is incredible. I can spot an expired registration sticker on a license plate on a car a quarter of a mile away. I'd make a great traffic cop!

I'm really good at mowing, because I use a pattern with very straight lines. And it's fun because the white noise of the mower helps me think more deeply and complexly. I do some really good thinking and planning on the mower.

I'm extremely sensitive to my environment, which helps me take perfect photographs, accurately predict changes in the weather, and determine what coin has been dropped in the grocery store by the sound it makes! I can also keep track of my energy level by listening to my body better than most people.

Having SPD makes it really easy for me to identify with and understand others with SPD. I can connect with them, draw them out, and easily cut them slack when they need it. When I was about six, my mom took me to play with another kid who had never talked to anyone outside their house. Well, he talked to me! His mother was completely shocked. It made him comfortable enough, I guess, when all I did was be me.

Looking toward my future, I'm confident that I could be assured a position at any job I aim for, and could likely do well at that job with enough experience and hard work. But why stop there, when I could take a more rigorous route and become prepared to excel, perhaps even beyond the scope of my original hopes?

NOT AFRAID ANYMORE TO STAND OUT
EMBER WALKER

By the time I was a senior in high school, I realized what a gift SPD could be. If I chose to look back, I could see how I'd adapted, changed, and coped with the various things that popped up. I could see that this thing, which at the time I had no name for, had actually made me a stronger person and more firm in my belief of who I was and what I stood for. I was not afraid anymore to stand out in the crowd and had no need to follow the crowd, either. I had learned to advocate for myself. I still had some years before I felt completely comfortable doing it, but I learned how to stand on my own two feet.

SPD HAS BEEN A GIFT
JASON FISCH

SPD is a roller coaster. There are great days and there are bad ones. With a very supportive, loving family (and hours and hours of therapies of all sorts) I have learned that my SPD has been a gift.

Growing up with all my sensitivities, I have learned to be compassionate. I have learned that, although not all other kids had SPD, they reacted the same way that I would to some situations. They would be hurt if kids were picking on them. They would feel left out if they weren't invited to a party. If I don't want to feel that way, why would anybody else? I knew if someone had a problem, I could relate. I think that I could help other people cope with their problems and insecurities because I have already felt those feelings, maybe even a little stronger. In the end, all the hard work pays off.

True, sensory processing disorder can be an enormous burden for many children, adolescents, and young adults. But their perceptions often change as they grow up, become able to cope with adversity, and learn that the future is full of hope and possibilities. For these writers, SPD has not disabled them; it has enabled them to live a good life, one that may have seemed unimaginable during their childhoods.

TO LIVE WHAT CAN TRULY BE CALLED LIFE
GINA BETECH

In my teenage world, the words were: "No, I can't, I can't bear it, I'm afraid, it's dangerous, please go slowly, it's too loud, too bright, too hot, too noisy. Don't move, don't make me move." Anxiety was my natural state; I perceived what others did not; I never knew what my mood would be tomorrow or even at a later hour. Just to live was difficult. But I grew up, and I got help, and I got better.

I have learned that SPD has two faces. One we know and struggle with, and the other we can recognize when we become steady and are ready to discover a magnificent gift: Sensitivity. Sensitivity makes me suffer so much but also gives me so much—an opportunity to connect with my inner world, my body, and my sensations; to experience my surroundings and nature; to know what other people are feeling; and to have a superior awareness, a special intensity, about things that just we can see and others cannot, as we interpret the world through a unique filter.

Young adults—and children who will become adults—need to know the most important thing about SPD: With work and help, it is possible to learn and accept that yes, you are different—not a bad different, but a good different. It is possible to conquer SPD and to live what can truly be called Life.

The contributors who volunteered to share their experiences in this book amaze me. I am so proud of them and love them so much! I thank them for writing and you, dear readers, for reading. I feel privileged to bring you together. I hope the strategies and insights covered help even more out-of-sync kids grow into in-sync young adults.

STRATEGIES FOR COPING WITH SENSORY PROCESSING DISORDER

In gathering these stories and writing this book, I sought to learn how children learn to cope with SPD as they develop into adolescents and young adults. I believe that developing coping skills to live successfully is based on several components.

Support from Within

These internal strategies, which develop over time, relate to self-awareness. With these the adolescent has a head start.

- Making choices about one's sensory lifestyle, including one's preferred foods, clothing, daily regimen, pace of life, social situations, home and work environments—choices that may not have been possible to make during childhood.

- Developing self-regulation in order to manage activities of daily living—dressing, eating, getting out the door, sleeping, and so forth. Also, developing self-control to tolerate temporary discomfort for the sake of desirable outcomes, because one knows that going shopping or to the dentist is necessary and won't last long.

- Accepting oneself, quirks and all, and taking ownership of SPD, while recognizing that sensory challenges may endure as one continues to grow.

- Being determined to connect socially with others, make conversation, and maintain friendships.

- Becoming passionate about what one wants to do, what causes one is willing to fight for, and who one strives to be.

- Developing the physical and mental ability to practice, practice, practice to achieve one's goals.

- Looking outward with compassion and using one's extrasensory grace, strengths, and special gifts to be mindful of others and improve their lives.

Support from Others

These external strategies relate to the awareness of other people. With these the adolescent with SPD will have an even greater chance to function smoothly and succeed in life.

- An observant, attentive parent or family that becomes knowledgeable about an adolescent or young adult's sensory processing difficulties, *really listens*, and problem-solves together to make effective changes.
- Understanding and support from educators who are willing to make changes in the school environment so it is more conducive to learning.
- Appropriate and effective therapy, finely tuned to the adolescent or young adult's individual sensory needs.
- Public awareness of sensory processing disorder and how it may affect adolescents and young adults—and everyone in their circle.

Onward!

ACKNOWLEDGMENTS

Primarily, I thank the story writers—adolescents and young adults with SPD, mature adults looking back, and family members—for bringing this book to life. (Read about them at the end of the book.) I am grateful to Lucy Jane Miller, PhD, and Lindsey Biel for considering every word of the manuscript and contributing their work; Joye Newman, Julia Berry, Nancy McManus, and Polly Panitz, MD, for their "why-didn't-I-think-of-that" suggestions; Laurence Steinberg, PhD, Deborah Shulman, and Jennifer Pleasure, PsyD, for their guidance about adolescent development; Kelly Dorfman, Peter Sullivan, and Minna Loketch Fischer for their expert contributions; and Cantor Rachel Hersh for exploring with me the topic of grace. I thank Mark Zweig for his encouragement, mindfulness, patience, love, and so much more.

Special thanks go to my sister Ellen Stern and Rachel S. Schneider for being there as we wrote our books, virtually side by side.

I shall always be indebted to Lynn Sonberg and Meg Schneider of Skylight Press and thank Meg also for her coping tips. And I thank Marian Lizzi, my TarcherPerigee editor who has worked with me on three other "Sync" books and knew I could write this one, too.

—Carol Stock Kranowitz
Bethesda, Maryland
Spring 2016

APPENDIX:
About the People in This Book

ADOLESCENTS AND YOUNG ADULTS

These are their names, the ages they were when they (or their parents) wrote for this book, and what they are doing now.

Lecia Baker (eighteen years old) lives in Georgia, where she copes with her SPD and pursues a degree in interpreting American Sign Language.

Kylie Boazman (twenty-one) has received a master's in sociology and anthropology and is working on a second master's in disability studies. She hopes to become an anthropology professor and disability activist.

Kori Cotteleer (twenty) has graduated from Iowa State University with a degree in animal ecology/preveterinary and a minor in biology. An Illinois native, she works at a nature center doing outreach education and at a wildlife rehabilitation center on Sanibel Island, Florida.

Hayley Fannin (nineteen) is a technical college graduate living in Washington State. She loves Disney movies and is on the path to find a permanent career, currently working and enjoying life with family and friends by her side.

Jason Fisch (fourteen) is a high school student, a champion on the basketball court and in the classroom, and involved in volunteering in his community and especially for STAR Institute. He lives with his family and dog Bronco in Colorado.

Andrew Herbert (twelve) lives in Texas and is now a professor of music composition at a community college.

Ian Hoyman (fourteen) lives in Colorado. He is a writer and loves reading, his dog Ripley, and playing the bass viol by himself and with his father, a bassoonist.

Michael Jacobs (eighteen), as a little boy, had severe auditory over-responsivity, was afraid of stairs, and didn't ride a bike until age nine, after four years of OT. Today, he is a U.S. Marine, Assault Climber/Infantry Unit, and is studying criminal justice. He was raised in New Hampshire.

Karly Koop (eighteen) teaches kindergarten and first grade in a homeschool co-op and runs the Wiggle Room (a sensorimotor lab) at an elementary school near her Texas home. She is learning American Sign Language and to play the piano. She has earned a brown belt in karate, her passion.

Kevin Larson (fifteen) has SPD and autism (and calls himself an "autist"). He lives in South Carolina and is currently an honors student at Texas A&M University, where he's majoring in meteorology and minoring in physics and mathematics. He is a National Merit Scholar, a member of the Phi Eta National Honor Society, a student mentor, a member of TAMSCAMS (the university's chapter of the

American Meteorological Society), and on the Honors Student Council. His interests include cartography, numismatics, languages, and Mario Kart DS speedrunning.

Kerry Magro (twenty-five) is a motivational speaker, talk show host, film consultant, and advocate for people with autism, SPD, and other disabilities. He wrote *Defining Autism from the Heart* and *Autism and Falling in Love* and contributed to *College for Students with Disabilities: We Do Belong*. He has a master's in strategic communication from Seton Hall University and lives in New Jersey.

Bob Palmer (twenty-one) is the subject of his wife Melissa's story. Now he is a loving husband and wonderful father to two girls with sensory issues of their own.

Daisy Roberg (eighteen) is the subject of her mother's story. The family lives in New Jersey.

Chloe Rothschild (eighteen) is an autism advocate living in Ohio.

Leanna Taylor (sixteen) is currently majoring in forensic science at Loyola University in Chicago. Her home is Maryland.

Daniel Travis (twenty-four) lives in Michigan and is a Web developer. He also runs websites offering support to those struggling with SPD. He loves music, writes comedic fiction, and tries to make a positive impact in every life he touches.

Justin Wayland (sixteen) is enrolled in a science and technology magnet program at a Maryland high school. He enjoys petting his cats and programming and wants to be a computer scientist.

Lydia Wayman (twenty-four) lives in Pennsylvania and holds an MA in English and nonfiction writing. Lydia advocates for the autism community through speaking, writing, and visual arts. She is cowriting a novel with an autistic main character for middle-schoolers. She loves cats and being creative.

Tyler Ann Whitney (fourteen) lives in Oklahoma and loves school, softball, theater, judo, karate, and witty TV sitcoms. Her dream job when she grows up is to work at the Smithsonian Institution in Washington, DC, as a forensic anthropologist.

Shalea Wilson (twelve) is the subject of her mother Deb's story. Now Shalea attends a transition academic program in Washington State and works for S'cool Moves, assembling educational kits. She helps to educate others about SPD by participating in demonstration videos shared with educators and therapists.

ADULTS LOOKING BACK AT THEIR ADOLESCENCE

Laurie Appel, OTR/L, practices occupational therapy with a sensory integration approach at her clinic, the Lotus Tree, in Idaho. She considers herself "a sensory kid, all grown up."

Bob Argue works full time to help homeless people and families pay for affordable housing in rural SW Michigan. He serves on the Board of Directors of Disability Network Southwest Michigan. His dating life has improved, thanks to reconnecting with a high school crush who has similar sensory problems.

Paul Balius works as the IT director of applications for a large national firm. For fourteen years he volunteered in the prison ministry in multiple California prisons and continues counseling and preaching in a home church. He is writing his first book.

Gina Betech lives in Mexico, where she cares for her family, learns about the mind-body-psyche connection, and practices somatic movement, Pilates, and yoga. Through intensive therapy she has experienced amazing improvement in the way she inhabits her own being and relates to the world.

Meredith Joseph Blaine, living in Kentucky, has an MS in library and information science with a special interest in issues related to ASD, SPD, and neuroscience. He wants to receive more fun and playful sensory therapies one day, both in an OT gym and in an indoor trampoline park.

Mary Ann Conway lives in New Jersey. She is a photographer, artist, and craftswoman and considers herself a giver, not a taker. Sensory issues still bother her, but she has developed her teenage interests and today enjoys a satisfying career as a graphic artist, crafter, photographer, and desktop publisher.

Debbie Feely lives in California, focusing now on grandkids and church activities. She is a homeschool adviser, speaker, and writer. Although she did not receive treatment for SPD as a child, she learned later about how effective it can be and practiced for ten years as a perceptual-motor therapist.

Marlene Gomez, OTR and psychologist, treats children and adults in Mexico City. She is a professor of psychosocial OT and human development in the Instituto de Terapia Ocupacional. One of her specialties is understanding how teenagers with eating issues may resort to unusual behaviors, and what to help them do so they can live and socialize with more satisfaction.

Temple Grandin, PhD, writes and speaks about her struggles and successes as a person with autism and as a designer of livestock-handling equipment. She is a professor of animal science at Colorado State University. Her many books include *Temple Talks . . . about Autism and Sensory Issues* (2015) and *The Autistic Brain* (2013).

Annette Himmelreich, LMSW, a teacher and social worker, lives in Texas. She has worked with traumatized children, adolescents, and adults in a variety of care facilities in the United States and Russia. She teaches English as a Second Language and works with those who have gone through grief and loss.

Joanna Lees lives in Indiana with her godmother and a pack of dogs, one cat, and too many wild birds and critters to count. She currently works in property and casualty insurance. She plans to take swim lessons.

Shonda Lucas lives in Kentucky with her adopted son. She is active on inclusion and disabilities boards, speaks about special education at the University of Kentucky and in the special needs community, and advocates for adoptive parents of children with SPD and other developmental issues.

Judy McCarter, OTR/L, speaks about SPD and other issues and practices SI in her clinic, Functional Therapy, in Oklahoma. She is still evolving and understanding her gifts with the help of Benny, her service dog.

Jennifer McIlwee Myers was diagnosed with Asperger's syndrome[1] at the age of thirty-six. She refers to herself as the "Aspie at Large." She lives in California with her husband and is the author of *Growing Up with Sensory Issues: Insider Tips from a Woman with Autism*.

Zachary Prossick-Brown received therapy as a boy and copes effectively by quiet time alone, physical action (cycling, running, and weightlifting), producing art, and socializing with friends. He lives in Texas and works as a crew leader for a custodial team.

---

1   Asperger's syndrome is no longer a diagnosis in the fifth edition of the *Diagnostic and Statistical Manual of Mental Disorders* (*DSM-5*) (2013). It has been absorbed into autism spectrum disorder (ASD).

Christopher Sabine, LICSW, has optic nerve hypoplasia (ONH) and is significantly visually impaired. Living in Ohio, he is president of ONH Consulting, which provides support, consultation, and advocacy services to families of children with ONH and related conditions.

Rachel S. Schneider, MA, MHC, is an SPD community advocate with a background in mental health counseling and author of *Making Sense: A Guide to Sensory Issues* (2016). Diagnosed with SPD at age twenty-seven, she chronicles her journey at www.comingto senses.blogspot.com. She lives in New York with her husband.

Charles Shidlofsky, OD, FCOVD, a native New Yorker, now lives and practices optometry in the Dallas, Texas, area.

Andrew Short lives in Canberra, Australia. He has cerebral palsy and is always looking for ways to improve his sensory functioning. He provided a number of strategies for coping with SPD and offers more at http://blindsensoryexploration.com/.

Ember Walker lives in Nebraska with her husband and their two sons, both of whom have SPD.

Nicole Anson Wolske lives in Massachusetts and is studying to be a pediatric occupational therapist.

FAMILY MEMBERS

Aaron Fisch and Marla Roth-Fisch, Jason's parents, live in Colorado. Aaron is in the hospitality industry; Marla is a digital marketing consultant. Both do advocacy work for SPD. Marla is a board member of STAR Institute and is an award-winning author/illustrator of two children's books, *Sensitive Sam* and *Sensitive Sam Visits the Dentist*.

Abigayle Fisch, who was fifteen when she contributed her thoughts to this book, is Jason's sister. She is a high school honor student, active in dance and fitness, leadership, and volunteering in her community and for STAR Institute.

Sally Herbert, Andrew's mother, is a speech-and-language pathologist and owner of a clinic in Texas that specializes in children with auditory processing disorders and children on the autism spectrum. She is writing a book about Andrew entitled *I've Never Known Silence*.

Melissa Palmer, Bob's wife, teaches college and writes books when she's not wrangling pets or "momming." She is the author of *A Life Less Normal*. The family lives in New Jersey, close enough to the beach to enjoy it, and far enough away to avoid the noise and crowds.

Avigail Roberg and her family, including daughter Daisy, live in New Jersey.

Bobbi Sheahan, a former assistant district attorney, is now a full-time mother in Texas. She was an editor at *Future Horizons*, writes a column for *Sensory Focus* magazine, and is on the advisory board of *Autism Asperger's Digest*. Sensory issues are among the many things that she and her husband and kids have in common. She has coauthored three books, including *What I Wish I'd Known about Raising a Child with Autism*.

Peter Sullivan is an environmental health researcher focusing on toxins and wireless safety, as well as the father of two sons who used to have serious sensory issues. The family lives in California. See www.clearlightventures.com for more.

Lisa Wunderlich Taylor, MEd, is a learning specialist and parent of four teenagers with SPD, living in Maryland. She works with students of all ages to realize their potential. She provides academic therapy at Imagine Possibility, www.iptutoring.com.

Debra Em Wilson, who writes about herself and her daughter Shalea, is a neurodevelopmental learning specialist and founder of S'cool Moves, a company whose mission is to educate people about learning differences and create job opportunities for adolescents and adults with disabilities. The family lives in Washington State.

SPECIALISTS

Lindsey Biel, MA, OTR/L, has a private practice in New York City where she evaluates and treats children and adolescents with ASD and other developmental challenges. She is coauthor of *Raising a Sensory Smart Child: The Definitive Handbook for Helping Your Child with Sensory Processing Issues* and author of *Sensory Processing Challenges: Effective Clinical Work with Kids and Teens*. Her website is www.sensorysmarts.com.

Kelly Dorfman, MS, LND, a clinical nutritionist, lives in Maryland. She uses nutrition therapeutically to improve brain function, energy, and mood. She has helped many children and adolescents with a cornucopia of eating issues. Her recent book is *Cure Your Child with Food*. See www.kellydorfman.com.

Minna Loketch Fischer, MS, lives in New York. With a background in mental health counseling, she is completing her Doctorate in Psychology at Hofstra University. Minna's clinical focus is on helping children, adolescents, and their families cope with the cognitive and psychosocial impact of medical diagnoses. She is currently a psychology intern at Winthrop University Hospital.

Lucy Jane Miller, PhD, OTR, lives in Colorado. She is Founder of STAR Institute for Sensory Processing Disorder in Denver. She is the author of *Sensational Kids: Hope and Help for Children with SPD* and coauthor of *No Longer A SECRET: Unique Common Sense Strategies for Children with Sensory or Motor Challenges*. See www .spdstar.org.

Stephanie J. Whitney, OTR/L, who writes about her daughter, Tyler Ann, works in schools and pediatric outpatient settings with an emphasis in sensory integration. The family lives in Oklahoma.

GLOSSARY

Cognitive behavioral therapy (CBT): a talking therapy to help one manage problems by altering one's thinking and behavioral patterns

Extrasensory grace: Coming from within a person, an intrinsic, elegant, spirited, superior talent (e.g., dancing, singing, speaking, or writing) or quality (e.g., extraordinary compassion for other people's feelings and needs).

Gravitational insecurity: Sensation that you will fall when your head position changes or when you move through space, as when scaling a ladder or riding an escalator.

IEP: Individualized Education Program, specifying the needs of a student identified as having a learning disability and providing for special education and related services.

In sync: Adapting smoothly to changes, moving easily, working effectively with objects, and participating harmoniously with people in your environment.

Just right: Expression used by A. Jean Ayres, PhD, OTR, in her talks to denote an appropriate, functional, and satisfying sensory or motor challenge.

Meltdown: Response to sensory overstimulation or anticipated overstimulation, especially related to a change in expectations, usually accompanied by a tantrum and copious tears; may be characterized by intense anger or fear.

Metacognition: Awareness and comprehension of one's own thought processes; "thinking about thinking."

Misophonia: Literally, "hatred of sound," a disorder in which a specific sound, such as chewing, slurping, or breathing, triggers a negative emotion like anger, a flight urge, or disgust.

Motor plan: Organization and sequencing of the steps of an unfamiliar and complex action in a coordinated manner.

Movement quota: Fixed amount of physical activity an individual needs each day.

Multisensory integration: Processing in the brain of simultaneous stimuli from various sensory systems to help a person accurately perceive what is in the environment, e.g., seeing and rubbing sandpaper, or touching and hearing synthetic fabric.

Neurotypical: A person who is not on the autism spectrum.

Not OK: Uncomfortable or intolerable.

Out of sync: Not working well, or not working at the same time and speed as other people.

Seeking sync: Striving to adapt smoothly to transitions and sensory challenges in order to function well and participate fully in daily life.

Sensory lifestyle: An individual's way of living that incorporates—or eliminates—sensory stimuli to help the person function smoothly in daily life. It includes healthful eating, sleeping, vigorous activity, and interactions with people and the environment.

Sensory processing disorder (SPD): A neurophysiological condition in which one's brain inefficiently detects, modulates, or interprets sensory input from one's body or from the environment. Too much or not enough sensory stimulation may cause atypical movement, emotions, attention, relationships, and behavioral responses. For definitions of SPD's categories and subtypes, refer to chapter 2 ("Primer") or see *The Out-of-Sync Child: Recognizing and Coping with SPD*, revised (2005).

Shutdown: Sudden sleepiness or inertia as a response to sensory overstimulation; may be characterized by fear or by dissociation, i.e., the feeling that you or your environment is unreal.

Synesthesia: Neurological phenomenon in which input into one sensory system, such as hearing, simultaneously stimulates another sense, such as vision.

Weighted blanket or garment: Blanket, vest, or jacket with weights sewn in or placed in pockets to help calm and focus individuals with sensory issues.

White noise: Sound created by a continuum of frequencies distributed equally over the entire hearing range. Portable white noise machines can decrease sensitivity to environmental sounds and mask background noises to help people study, work, and sleep.

REFERENCES

Ben-Sasson, A., A. S. Carter, and M. J. Briggs-Gowan. 2009. Sensory over-responsivity in elementary school: Prevalence and social-emotional correlates. *Journal of Abnormal Child Psychology* 37 (5): 705–16.

Bushdid, C., M. O. Magnasco, L. B. Vosshall, and A. Keller. 2014. Humans can discriminate more than 1 trillion olfactory stimuli. *Science* 343 (6177): 1370–72.

Campbell, J. 1991. *The Power of Myth*. New York: Anchor.

Chein, J., L. Steinberg, et al. 2011. Peers increase adolescent risk taking by enhancing activity in the brain's reward circuitry. *Developmental Science* 14 (2): F1–10.

Dorfman, K. Various articles about picky eating, magnesium and zinc, how sensory processing and nutrition interact, and other nutritional issues originally published in *New Developments*, the quarterly newsletter of the nonprofit Developmental Delay Resources, are still available at http://devdelay.org/newsletter/articles/html/. See www .EpidemicAnswers.org for additional articles.

Grandin, T. 2006. *Thinking in Pictures: My Life with Autism*, expanded ed. New York: Vintage. Also *Temple Grandin*, 2010, HBO video, http://fhautism.com/temple-grandin-hbo-award-winning-dvd .html.

Magro, K. *Defining Autism from the Heart* (2013) and *Autism and Falling in Love: To the One That Got Away* (2014). Self-published; available through Amazon.com.

Miller, L. J., M. E. Anzalone, S. J. Lane, S. A. Cermak, and E. T. Osten. 2007. Concept evolution in sensory integration: A proposed nosology for diagnosis. *American Journal of Occupational Therapy* 61 (2): 135–40.

Sheahan, B. 2014. I feel (sort of) pretty. *Autism Asperger's Digest* (May–June): 18–19. http://autismdigest.com/aadigest-may-june -2014/.

Starseed, S. P. 2011. *The Ecology of Learning: Re-Inventing Schools.* Richmond, VA: In-Sync Therapy.

Steinberg, L. 2012. Should the science of adolescent brain development inform public policy? *Issues in Science and Technology* 28 (3): 3.

Sullivan, P. Various articles about wireless radiation, electromagnetic fields, and other environmental stressors at www.clearlightventures .com

Travis, D. 2009. Five steps for dealing with SPD as an adult. *S.I. Focus* (Spring).

Wilson, D. E., and M. C. Heiniger-White. 2014. *S'cool Moves for Learning: Enhance Learning through Self-Regulation Activities.* Shasta, CA: Integrated Learner Press.

SUGGESTED READING

Bialer, D. S., and L. J. Miller. 2011. *No Longer A SECRET: Unique Common Sense Strategies for Children with Sensory or Motor Challenges.* Arlington, TX: Sensory World.

Biel, L. 2014. *Sensory Processing Challenges: Effective Clinical Work with Kids and Teens.* New York: W. W. Norton.

———, and N. Peske. 2009. *Raising a Sensory Smart Child: The Definitive Handbook for Helping Your Child with Sensory Processing Issues,* revised. (See chapter 15, "The Special Challenges for Teenagers.")

Dalgliesh, C. 2013. *The Sensory Child Gets Organized: Proven Systems for Rigid, Anxious, or Distracted Kids.* New York: Simon and Schuster.

Dorfman, K. 2011. *Cure Your Child with Food: The Hidden Connections between Nutrition and Childhood Ailments.* New York: Workman.

Golomb, R.G. and S. Mouton-Odom, 2016. *Psychological Interventions for Children with Sensory Dysregulation.* New York: Guilford.

Grandin, T. 2011. *The Way I See It: A Personal Look at Autism and Asperger's,* revised. Arlington, TX: Future Horizons. (See chapter 3, "Sensory Issues.")

———. 2015. *Temple Talks . . . about Autism and Sensory Issues.*
Arlington, TX: Sensory World.

Healy, J. M. 2004. *Your Child's Growing Mind: Brain Development and
Learning from Birth to Adolescence.* New York: Harmony.

———. 2010. *Different Learners: Identifying, Preventing, and Treating
Your Child's Learning Problems.* New York: Simon and Schuster.

Heller, S. 2003. *Too Loud, Too Bright, Too Fast, Too Tight: What to Do If
You Are Sensory Defensive in an Overstimulating World.* New York:
Harper Perennial.

Henry, D., T. Wheeler, and D. I. Sava. 2004. *Sensory Integration Tools
for Teens: Strategies to Promote Sensory Processing.* Flagstaff, AZ:
Henry OT Services.

Kashman, N., and J. Mora. 2005. *The Sensory Connection: An OT and
SLP Team Approach*, revised. Arlington, TX: Sensory World. (See
chapter 8, "Strategies for the Adult and Older Child.")

Kranowitz, C. S. 2005. *The Out-of-Sync Child: Recognizing and Coping
with Sensory Processing Disorder*, 2nd ed. New York: Perigee.

———. 2010. *The Goodenoughs Get in Sync: Five Family Members
Overcome Their Special Sensory Issues.* Arlington, TX: Sensory
World.

Lemer, P. S., ed. 2014. *Outsmarting Autism: The Ultimate Guide to
Management, Healing, and Prevention.* Tarentum, PA: World
Association Publishers.

Miller, L. J. 2014. *Sensational Kids: Hope and Help for Children with
Sensory Processing Disorder*, 2nd ed. New York: Perigee. (See
chapter 10, "As Sensational Children Grow Up.")

Mucklow, N. 2009. *The Sensory Team Handbook: A Hands-On Tool to
Help Young People Make Sense of Their Senses and Take Charge of
Their Sensory Processing*, 2nd ed. Kingston, Ontario: Michael
Grass.

Myers, J. M. 2014. *Growing Up with Sensory Processing Disorder: Insider
Tips from a Woman with Autism.* Arlington, TX: Sensory World.

Myles, B. S., et al. 2002. *Asperger Syndrome and Sensory Issues: Practical Solutions for Making Sense of the World.* Shawnee Mission, KS: Autism Asperger.

Schneider, R. S. 2016. *Making Sense: A Guide to Sensory Issues.* Arlington, TX: Sensory World. Also see *The Sensational Struggle and Success of SPD Teenagers* (March 2015), at www.comingtosenses.blogspot.com.

Steinberg, L. 2014. *Age of Opportunity: Lessons from the New Science of Adolescence.* New York: Eamon Dolan/Houghton Mifflin Harcourt.

Voss, A. 2013. *Your Essential Guide to Understanding Sensory Processing Disorder,* 2nd ed. CreateSpace Independent Publishing.

Also see scholarly articles and research papers about SPD in adolescents and adults in professional journals, in *OT Practice*, in *AOTA's Sensory Integration Special Interest Section* newsletters, and on the Internet. Researchers include Moya Kinnealey, PhD, Lucy Jane Miller, PhD, Sarah A. Schoen, PhD, Tina Champagne, OTD, Teresa May-Benson, ScD, Beth Pfeiffer, PhD, and the late Jane Koomar, PhD.

RESOURCES

For information about equipment mentioned in this book and much more, please refer to www.sensorysmarts.com, www.therapro.com, and other Internet sites.

STAR Institute for Sensory Processing Disorder

5420 S. Quebec Street, Suite 103
Greenwood Village, CO 80111
Telephone: (303) 221-7827 (221-STAR)
Fax: (303) 322-5550
E-mail: info@spdstar.org
Website: www.spdstar.org

Serving children and adults with SPD and their families by leading the field in SPD treatment, research, and education. STAR Institute is the world's most comprehensive and accurate (research-based) source of information about SPD from each of its three centers:

STAR Institute for SPD
Treatment Center

The premier treatment facility for children diagnosed with SPD and/or other developmental and behavioral conditions that include significant sensory issues. Services include:

- Multidiscipline team offering multidisciplinary evaluations (MD, psychologist, OT, speech and language, and family functioning)
- Evidence-based OT with a focus on regulation, relationships, and sensory integration clinical reasoning
- Unique STAR "Intensive Burst" treatment model developed by Dr. Lucy Jane Miller that offers five-day-a-week, short-term therapy for out-of-town families
- Extensive parent education, family support, and coaching offered individually and in groups, integrated into child's holistic treatment program
- Family training in problem solving so parents can integrate therapeutic ideas into daily life to reinforce the benefits of direct intensive therapy
- Treatment collaboration with a full suite of professionals, including speech/language therapy, pediatrics, psychology, and parent counseling
- Therapies including the family-centered Sequential Oral Sensory (SOS) approach to feeding; Integrated Listening Systems (iLs); and developmental, individual-differences, and relationship-based approach (DIR/Floortime)
- A program, new in 2016, just for adults and adolescents with SPD, that takes a multidisciplinary approach to treatment. Treatment is often a consultation

model with short-term advice and support, which is especially useful for out-of-town clients. Often the evaluation is in person with short-term treatment options and follow-up by Skype, Zoom, or other online methods

- National SPD Treatment Directory—listing for treatment providers in ten categories, such as OTs, SLPs, and MDs

STAR Institute for SPD
Research Center

Serving children with SPD and their families by leading research to advance the diagnosis and treatment of SPD through:

- Research—full-time program of SPD scientific study, directed by Dr. Lucy Jane Miller

STAR Institute for SPD
Education Center

Providing resources and education for families, therapists, educators, and physicians to expand knowledge, foster awareness, and promote recognition of SPD. Education opportunities include:

- SPD University—e-learning with over seventy online classes and resources (CEUs available)
- SPD Parent Connections—community-based, national, and international family education organizations
- Intensive Mentorships—small-group training opportunities for professionals
- Annual international symposiums and institutes

- Library—hundreds of clinical articles and other SPD information, free and accessible online
- Diagnostic Advocacy—spearheading the movement for acceptance of SPD as a valid diagnosis, with eighteen years of advocacy for inclusion in the Diagnostic and Statistical Manual of Mental Disorders, fifth edition (DSM-5) and currently with Zero to Three Diagnostic Manual

Sensory Focus magazine

Formerly called *S.I. Focus*, the magazine is devoted to "understanding the issues behind the behavior." Digital and print format issues available at www.sensoryworld.com.

Writers' Websites and Blogs

Lindsey Biel
www.sensorysmarts.com

Kelly Dorfman
www.kellydorfman.com

Rachel S. Schneider
www.comingtosenses.blogspot.com

Andrew Short
http://blindsensoryexploration.com/

Peter Sullivan
www.clearlightventures.com

Daniel Travis
www.spdlife.org

INDEX

ABOUT THE AUTHOR

Photo by Doug Bolst

Carol Stock Kranowitz, an early education teacher for twenty-five years, observed many out-of-sync preschoolers. To help them become more competent in their work and play, she began to study sensory integration (SI) theory. She learned to help identify their needs and steer them into intervention. In her workshops and writings, she explains to parents, educators, and other professionals how sensory processing disorder plays out in children and teenagers—and provides practical and enjoyable techniques for addressing sensory issues at home and school.

A graduate of Barnard College, Carol has an MA in education and human development from the George Washington University. She is a board member of STAR Institute in Colorado. She lives in Bethesda, Maryland, plays the cello, and has two married sons and five enchanting grandchildren.

Carol's other publications include:

- *The Out-of-Sync Child: Recognizing and Coping with Sensory Processing Disorder*, 2nd ed. (New York: Perigee, 2005)
- *The Out-of-Sync Child Has Fun: Activities for Kids with Sensory Processing Disorder*, 2nd ed. (New York: Perigee, 2006)
- *Growing an In-Sync Child: Simple, Fun Activities to Help Every Child Develop, Learn, and Grow*, coauthored with Joye Newman (New York: Perigee, 2010)
- *The Goodenoughs Get in Sync: Five Family Members Overcome Their Special Sensory Issues*, revised (Arlington, TX: Sensory World, 2010)
- *101 Activities for Kids in Tight Spaces* (New York: St. Martin's Press, 1995)

For more information, visit: www.out-of-sync-child.com.

Also from
Carol Kranowitz

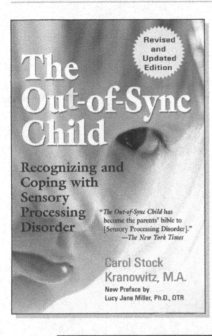

Revised and Updated Edition

The Out-of-Sync Child

Recognizing and Coping with Sensory Processing Disorder

"*The Out-of-Sync Child* has become the parents' bible to [Sensory Processing Disorder]."
—*The New York Times*

Carol Stock Kranowitz, M.A.
New Preface by Lucy Jane Miller, Ph.D., OTR

From the bestselling author of
The Out-of-Sync Child

Growing an In-Sync Child

Simple, Fun Activities to Help Every Child Develop, Learn, and Grow

Carol Kranowitz, M.A. and Joye Newman, M.A.

Foreword by Jane M. Healy, Ph.D., author of *Your Child's Growing Mind*

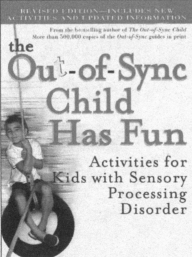

REVISED EDITION—INCLUDES NEW ACTIVITIES AND UPDATED INFORMATION

From the bestselling author of *The Out-of-Sync Child*
More than 500,000 copies of the *Out-of-Sync* guides in print

the Out-of-Sync Child Has Fun

Activities for Kids with Sensory Processing Disorder

Carol Stock Kranowitz, M.A.
Foreword by Trude Turnquist, Ph.D, O.T.R./L.